The Congress
of Vienna

MILESTONES
IN MODERN
WORLD HISTORY

1600 · · · 1750 · · ·

1940 · · · 2000

The Boer War

The Bolshevik
Revolution

The British
Industrial Revolution

The Chinese
Cultural Revolution

The Collapse of
the Soviet Union

The Congress of Vienna

The Cuban Revolution

D-Day and the
Liberation of France

The End of Apartheid
in South Africa

The Establishment
of the State of Israel

The French Revolution
and the Rise
of Napoleon

The Great Irish Famine

The Indian
Independence
Act of 1947

The Iranian Revolution

The Manhattan Project

The Marshall Plan

The Mexican
Revolution

The Treaty of Nanking

The Treaty of Versailles

The Universal
Declaration of
Human Rights

The Congress of Vienna

ALAN ALLPORT

CHELSEA HOUSE
An Infobase Learning Company

The Congress of Vienna

Chelsea House
An imprint of Infobase Learning
132 West 31st Street
New York, NY 10001

Library of Congress Cataloging-in-Publication Data

Allport, Alan, 1970–
The Congress of Vienna / by Alan Allport.
   p.   cm. — (Milestones in modern world history)
Includes bibliographical references and index.
ISBN 978-1-60413-497-1 (hardcover : alk. paper) 1. Congress of Vienna (1814–1815)—Juvenile literature. 2. Napoleonic Wars, 1800-1815—Juvenile literature. 3. Europe—Politics and government—1789–1815—Juvenile literature. I. Title.
DC249.A45 2009
940.2'72—dc22   2009022862

Chelsea House books are available at special discounts when purchased in bulk quantities for businesses, associations, institutions, or sales promotions. Please call our Special Sales Department in New York at (212) 967-8800 or (800) 322-8755.

You can find Chelsea House on the World Wide Web at http://www.infobaselearning.com.

Text design by Erik Lindstrom
Cover design by Alicia Post
Composition by Keith Trego
Cover printed by Bang Printing, Brainerd, Minn.
Book printed and bound by Bang Printing, Brainerd, Minn.
Date printed: September 2011
Printed in the United States of America

This book is printed on acid-free paper.

All links and Web addresses were checked and verified to be correct at the time of publication. Because of the dynamic nature of the Web, some addresses and links may have changed since publication and may no longer be valid.

CONTENTS

Europe in Turmoil

It was Corporal Lafontaine of the Engineers who did it. He had been left in charge of the bridge while his commanding officer struggled through the packed and chaotic streets to try to get orders from headquarters. Corporal Lafontaine knew that above all else he must prevent the enemy from pursuing his comrades in the retreating French army, who had been streaming across the White Elster River all morning. All he had to do was to set off the explosive charges strung along the bridge to blow it sky high. He was supposed to wait until the very last minute. How many of his fellow Frenchmen were still on the enemy's side of the river? How far away were the advancing Russians? Lafontaine could see little through the smoke and flames of the burning city. The crash of cannon fire deafened him. Dare he wait any longer? Suddenly, the bullets of Russian riflemen began whizzing past him and his handful of terrified engineers. That was enough; time to go. Lafontaine lit the fuse. The bridge disappeared in a flash of white light.

Without realizing it, the panicking corporal had stranded tens of thousands of friendly troops on the wrong side of the river. Stunned, the retreating soldiers watched as their last escape route was blown to pieces. Men, horses, wagons, and artillery pieces plunged into the river, all discipline breaking down as the frightened mob scrambled to cross to the safety of the far bank. Few made it. Many drowned, weighed down by their heavy uniforms and equipment; others were shot dead as they waded clumsily through the water. The little river was quickly jammed with the bodies of soldiers, animals, and the crush of cannons and carts. More than 23,000 French troops had to throw down their weapons and surrender. As night fell over the battle-torn streets of Leipzig, Germany, on Tuesday, October 19, 1813, it was clear that the Grand Army of Emperor Napoleon Bonaparte had suffered a bloody defeat. Indeed, it was to sound the death-knell of his continental empire.

Three days earlier, more than 500,000 soldiers had met on the outskirts of this sleepy little Saxon town to decide nothing less than the fate of Europe. On the one side was Napoleon I, the conqueror of kings, 44 years old and recognized as the most brilliant general since Alexander the Great. On the other side were the leaders of the Sixth Coalition, the grand alliance of European nations that had assembled to bring down the hated Bonaparte once and for all. The battle was an all-European affair. Though they were called French troops, at least half of Napoleon's soldiers were Germans, Italians, or Poles, recruited from the corners of his empire; the Sixth Coalition was made up of Russians, Austrians, Prussians, and Swedes. Leipzig was not to be named "the Battle of the Nations" for nothing. It was an auspicious affair. Two crowned monarchs—King Frederick-

An 1837 painting of Napoleon Bonaparte and Prince Józef Poniatowski at the Battle of Leipzig on October 19, 1813. Napoleon's loss here foretold the end of his European empire and the beginning of the end of a generation of warfare on the continent.

William III of Prussia and Czar Alexander I of Russia—had personally shown up to watch Napoleon's defeat.

For both Frederick-William and Alexander, revenge was sweet. In 1806, Napoleon had destroyed the Prussian army at the Battle of Jena and forced a humiliating peace treaty on the king. Then, in 1812, he had invaded Russia, burning Moscow to the ground. That campaign, however, had been Napoleon's greatest mistake. Underestimating how difficult it was going to be to keep an army of half a million fed and supplied along hundreds of miles of unpaved Russian roads, the French emperor had watched his troops die in droves from disease, hunger, and cold. In the disastrous winter retreat from Moscow, barely 10,000 of Napoleon's troops made it out of Russia alive. The following spring, he had recruited and trained a new army

NAPOLEON BONAPARTE (1769–1821)

Napoleon Bonaparte—"the little corporal" to his adoring soldiers, "the ogre" to the enemies who feared and abhorred him, the man destined to be emperor of France—was hardly French at all. He was born in 1769 on the Mediterranean island of Corsica, which had become a territory of France only the year before. Napoleon grew up in an Italian household and never learned to speak French without a strong foreign accent, something he remained self-conscious about all his life. It was only because his father was a minor nobleman that Napoleon was able to leave his isolated home and study at an elite military academy in Paris, where he was commissioned as an artillery lieutenant at the age of 16.

Under normal circumstances, with no great family wealth or prestige to assist him, the young soldier would probably have remained an obscure junior officer for good. The outbreak of the French Revolution in 1789, however, created opportunities for ambitious men. Napoleon rose rapidly through the ranks of the revolutionary army. His great opportunity came in 1795, when he broke up an antigovernment riot in Paris by firing his cannons into the crowd; the grateful revolutionary leaders promoted him to general and sent him to northern Italy to take over a foundering military campaign against the Austrians. Over the next year, in a series of brilliantly fought engagements, he

to defend his empire from the advancing Sixth Coalition; but now, with his last of his veteran troops crushed at Leipzig, Bonaparte was essentially finished. In six months he would be

led his small and ill-equipped army to victory, forcing the panicking Austrians to sue for peace. In 1799, Napoleon, by now the most famous and popular man in France, organized a coup against his own government. He became "First Consul" in what was supposed to be a ruling council of three, but quickly pushed his colleagues into the background. In 1804, he crowned himself emperor of France.

Over the next 10 years, Emperor Bonaparte smashed the armies of his Austrian, Prussian, and Russian adversaries and ruled over a reorganized Europe that stretched from Spain to Poland. Only his most persistent enemies, the British, safe in their island homeland, proved unconquerable. It was in order to try to choke off trade between Britain and Russia that pushed Napoleon to order his catastrophic march on Moscow in 1812, a defeat that shattered his veteran army and encouraged the occupied peoples of Europe to rebel against him. In April 1814, Napoleon abdicated his title and was exiled to the island of Elba, off the coast of Italy. Within a year, he returned to France to try to regain his imperial throne, but he was defeated at the Battle of Waterloo and was sent under close arrest to the remote South Atlantic outcrop of St. Helena, where he died in 1821.

Throughout the nineteenth century, Napoleon continued to haunt the European imagination. To traditionalists, he was the bogeyman who inspired dangerous dissent among the young and hotheaded; to romantics, he was the visionary "man of talent" who had humbled kings and princes by no more than his natural genius and his strength of personality.

forced to abdicate as enemy forces crossed the French frontier and marched in triumph toward Paris.

Even as news of the great victory at Leipzig spread across Europe, however, uncertainty about the future was growing. Yes, it looked as though Napoleon's fall was inevitable. Peace would return to the continent for the first time in 21 years, but for how long?

After all, this was the *Sixth* Coalition. Five times before the European nations had tried to band together to defeat France, but each time the alliance had fallen apart. Sometimes

THE BATTLE OF LEIPZIG

The clash between Napoleon's *Grand Armée* and the coalition army at Leipzig in October 1813 was not only the largest, but also the bloodiest battle of the whole war. At least 130,000 soldiers and civilians were killed or wounded in 100 hours of furious combat. A year later, the battlefield was still covered with the corpses of forgotten and unburied horses and men. It was such scenes of carnage that encouraged the allied delegates at the Congress of Vienna to try to create a lasting peace in Europe after Napoleon's fall. Here is an eyewitness account of the battle, published in London a few months after it took place:

> Night drew on; the vast field of battle became gradually enveloped in darkness, and the horizon was now illuminated by the flashes of the guns alone . . . The battle had lasted the whole day all around the city. The church-clocks struck six; and, as if all the parties had unanimously agreed to suspend at this moment the horrid work of slaughter, the last cannon shot was fired . . . Nothing

it had been due to military defeats, but more often because of diplomatic quarrels and disunion. It had been hard enough to persuade Russia, Austria, Prussia, and the other coalition members to cooperate even when their vital interests were at stake. It was going to prove even harder to get them to agree to conditions for a lasting peace.

All of the members of the coalition had made great sacrifices in blood and treasure to defeat Napoleon. Not surprisingly, they expected to receive compensation for their efforts. Who was going to pay? France was the obvious culprit, but

now was seen around the horizon but one immense circle of many thousand watch-fires. In all directions appeared blazing villages, and from their number might be inferred the havoc occasioned by this arduous day.

Its effects were still more plainly manifested when we descended into the streets. Thousands of wounded had poured in at all the gates, and every moment increased their numbers. Many had lost an arm or a leg, and yet limped along with pitiable moans. As for a dressing for their wounds, that was a thing which could not yet be thought of; the poor wretches had themselves bound up with some old rag or other as well as they were able. . . . The consequences were inevitable. Many, as might naturally be expected, perished, in the night, of hunger, agony, and cold. Their lot was enviable—they no longer needed any human assistance. What heart would not have bled at such scenes of horror!*

* Frederic Shoberl, *Narrative of the Most Remarkable Events which Occurred in and Near Leipzig, Immediately Before, During, and Subsequent To, the Sanguinary Series of Engagements Between the Allied Armies and the French, from the 14th to the 19th October, 1813* (London: R. Ackermann, 1814).

not all the coalition partners were interested in French territory. Russia wanted land in Eastern Europe, particularly in the ancient kingdom of Poland. Prussia, however, had vital interests there as well. Austria wanted to expand into Italy, but the other allies were not going to sit idly by and watch the Austrians gobble up rich lands that could make them too powerful. Finally, there were the British. They had not had any troops at Leipzig, but it was money from London that had paid for the armies of the Sixth Coalition. The British had not spent a quarter of a century fighting the French only to see another European power threaten the stability of Europe. Napoleon had not surrendered yet, but allied diplomats were already whispering and conspiring behind one another's backs.

No matter how greedy and ambitious they might have been, the rulers of Europe were frightened too. They had been fighting a war not just against Napoleon but also against the dangerous ideas stirred up by the French Revolution of 1789. These new ideas—liberalism, nationalism—had been spread by revolutionary conquests and had taken hold in the minds of the young. A generation of idealistic men and women were growing up who were no longer satisfied with the old way of doing things. To the crowned heads of Europe, these ideas were far more dangerous than Bonaparte's armies because they represented a threat to the very fabric of society. War had brought turmoil and confusion; it unleashed the unstoppable forces of *revolution*. Maybe it was too risky to play power games any more. Perhaps, if the kings and emperors could not agree to cooperate, they would all lose their heads as King Louis XVI of France had lost his.

THE CONGRESS

A year after the Battle of Leipzig, in October 1814, delegates from the members of the Sixth Coalition met in the Austrian capital, Vienna, to work out a way to organize a peaceful and stable Europe. It was called the Congress of Vienna, and the set of

The Congress of Vienna was an international conference held in 1814–1815 to remake Europe after fall of Napoleon Bonaparte. Great Britain, Austria, Prussia, and Russia were the four major powers at the Congress that discussed peace terms with France. Above, furnishings used during the Congress of Vienna.

principles and institutions agreed to there would become known to history as the Congress System. The Congress System was founded on an idea that was new to Europe: that nations should settle disputes not by war and intrigue, but by mutual agreement. The states that had defeated France would not, as they had in the past, simply dismantle their alliance now that their common enemy was beaten, but would agree to consult regularly and permanently on matters of international importance.

Many of the optimistic plans of the Congress's creators did not turn out as they had hoped. Only a few years after Napoleon's defeat, the former allies of the Sixth Coalition had already broken ranks, squabbling over territorial boundaries. They began to dispute whether they should intervene in the domestic affairs of smaller nations. After 1822, they stopped meeting as a single body. Attempts to prevent the spread of liberal and national ideas among the common people of Europe turned out to be futile. Still, for 99 years after the Congress of Vienna—a remarkable period of self-restraint—there were no major wars on the continent.

The basic principle that had originated in 1814, that nations should solve their disputes by collective consultation and agreement—in other words, that countries should act as an *international community* with shared values and interests rather than just a mob of warring rivals—would live on long after the original Congress System broke down. In the twentieth century, it inspired the creation of the United Nations and other security institutions such as the North Atlantic Treaty Organization (NATO). For all its weaknesses, the Congress of Vienna established the basic set of rules by which nations still engage with one another today.

The French
Revolution
and Napoleon's
Conquests

The morning of Monday, January 21, 1793, dawned cold and wet. At eight o'clock, a mounted guard of more than 1,200 horsemen drew up outside a bleak fortress prison in the center of Paris. A short, stout, balding, middle-aged man, dressed in a plain shirt and pants, passed through the main prison door and was helped into a waiting carriage. The carriage and its massed entourage of guards made its way across the city, surrounded on all sides by thousands of ordinary Parisians, many armed with pikes and muskets as though expecting sudden attack. The procession passed without incident, however, and after two hours it arrived at the Place de la Révolution, a city square today known as the Place de la Concorde. There the man got out of the carriage and, with his hands bound and his shirt draped open at the neck, he walked with a firm brisk step toward a large wooden platform that had been newly erected

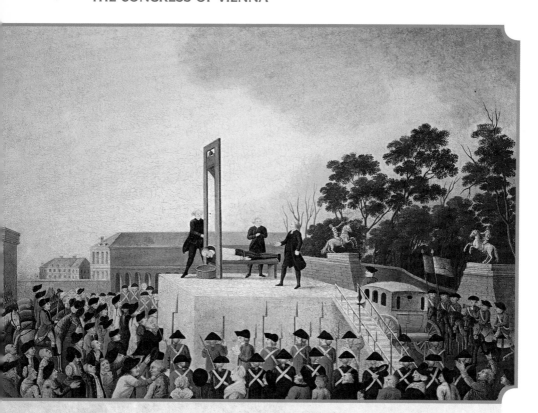

Seen here, the execution of Louis XVI, the former king of France, on January 21, 1793, during the French Revolution. The king's death would spark a quarter century of warfare on the European continent, beginning with the French Revolutionary Wars and continuing with the Napoleonic Wars.

in the middle of the square. On the platform was a tall upright frame with a huge, razor-sharp blade mounted on top. This was the newly invented device for the quick and painless public execution of the enemies of France—what would soon become known as the infamous Madame Guillotine.

The man—calm, dignified, and self-assured—mounted the platform and stared hard at the waiting assemblage of drummers until they ceased playing. Then, in the silence, he turned to the crowd and spoke in a loud, confident voice: "I die innocent of all the crimes laid to my charge. I pardon those who have occasioned my death. And I pray to God that the blood you are going to shed may never be visited on France."[1] Then he was led to the machine, his neck placed on the wooden execution block. It was all over in a second. A great roar came from the crowd as the decapitated head was held out. It was a quarter past ten. The people of France had killed their king.

The execution of King Louis XVI of the House of Bourbon was an event that would come to exemplify the bloody high drama of the French Revolution. Sadly, Louis's final wish did not come true. The violence that was visited upon him that January morning would be replicated millions of times over during the next 20 years, not only across France but throughout the rest of Europe too. The revolution, and the years of imperial conquest by Napoleon Bonaparte that immediately followed it, was perhaps concurrently the greatest, most awe-inspiring, and the most terrible series of events of the past 200 or so years. It certainly dominated the minds of the men who would meet at the Congress of Vienna in 1814. In order to understand them and what they were trying to accomplish there, it is necessary to know something about the French Revolution.

THE FALL OF THE OLD REGIME

France was the greatest country in Europe in 1789. It had the biggest population, the most powerful army, and its capital, Paris, was second only to London in size and magnificence. Culturally, France led the world. The French language was spoken at every royal court on the continent. France's painters, playwrights, and musicians were the model for high art. Its fashions set the style. French writers were the wittiest, French philosophers the most profound. France regarded itself—a bit pompously, but not without some justification—as being the center of the world.

France, however, was also a state deeply burdened by debt. Its long wars with England had ruined its finances. Though the French had successfully supported the American colonists' revolution in the 1770s, they had virtually bankrupted their own country in the process. The only way to redress this crisis would be to reform France's obsolete tax laws. That, however, would require King Louis XVI to call an Estates General—a grand assembly of the people—something that had not been done since 1614. His advisers were nervous. Would this taste of power go to the heads of king's subjects? Still, there was little choice. The proclamation went out: the Estates General would convene on May 5 to discuss reform of the nation's finances.

The Estates General was made up of three houses, representing the country's three estates: the clergy, the nobility, and the so-called Third Estate, i.e., the common people who made up 90 percent of the French population. When these three houses met at Louis's splendid palace at Versailles, near Paris, it was clear that the representatives of this third estate were not going to be content to talk about taxes alone. They had a chance to speak, at long last, and they were going to use it to the fullest. Ordinary Frenchmen had long been unhappy with the distribution of power within the country. Their labor produced the majority of its wealth, yet they were excluded from all political decision making. The Third Estate, which now began to call itself the National Assembly, demanded sweeping changes to the way that France was governed.

At first, the king and his nobles tried to bluff the commoners with vague promises. Then, on July 14, their bluff was called. A crowd of Parisians stormed the ancient royal fortress-prison known as the Bastille, a symbol of crown authority. Suddenly the pent-up frustration of France's masses could no longer be ignored. Louis lost his nerve and agreed to all the demands of the National Assembly. Almost without realizing it, the French had begun a revolution.

TERROR!

At first, the French Revolution seemed peaceful enough. Louis agreed to serve as a constitutional monarch, maintaining his throne but governing through an elected parliament just as the British king did. The National Assembly announced sweeping reforms, including a Declaration of the Rights of Man similar in tone to that of the American Declaration of Independence. Abroad, many statesmen looked at events in Paris with approval. Thomas Jefferson, the author of the Declaration of Independence, believed that "the liberty of the whole earth" depended upon the success of the revolutionaries in France.[2]

The peace, however, did not last. The king, who had never been sincere in his agreements with the revolutionaries, was soon plotting to resume absolute power. Angry noblemen were slipping across the border and forming secret armies to conquer France. Despite its best efforts, the National Assembly was unable to stabilize the ailing economy, and its decision to seize vast areas of land held by the Catholic Church caused religious tension throughout the country. Events soon gathered speed. A group of extremist revolutionaries known as the Jacobins gathered power in the Assembly. Louis and his family attempted to flee France, were caught, and were brought back to Paris under house arrest. Austria, whose emperor was King Louis's brother-in-law, protested; the National Assembly promptly declared war. In September 1791, the monarch was deposed and France declared itself a republic. Louis went on trial for his life and the National Assembly voted for his execution. Within a few months his wife, Queen Marie-Antoinette, would die by guillotine as well.

By September 1793, with foreign armies marching into France and civil war breaking out in areas such as the Vendée, the revolution seemed to be on the verge of collapse. Then a cold-eyed, fanatical, but brilliant young Jacobin named Maximilien Robespierre formed the dictatorial Committee of Public Safety. During the so-called Reign of Terror that lasted for the next 50 months, Robespierre and his colleagues used brute force to restore order to France. As many as 40,000 men, women, and children died in mass executions ordered by the committee. The world was horrified. Eventually Robespierre himself was arrested and was put to death. His Reign of Terror, however, saved the Revolution.

A BRUTAL CIVIL WAR

Not all Frenchmen rallied to the cause of revolution in 1789. In the Vendée region in the rural west of France, the peasants resented attempts by the revolutionary government in Paris to suppress the Catholic religion. Using hit-and-run guerrilla tactics, the so-called White counter-revolutionaries of the Vendée attacked and murdered local representatives of Robespierre's Committee of Public Safety. This is an account of the campaign by an ordinary Vendean soldier:

> Our army consisted of peasants like myself, wearing smocks or rough coats, armed with shotguns, pistols, muskets, often with tools—scythes, cudgels, axes, knives, and roasting spits. . . . We would march straight to the enemy, and having knelt to receive our priests' blessing, we would open fire at point-blank range, no doubt rather irregular, but well sustained and well aimed. As soon as we saw the Republican gunners about to open fire we would fling ourselves flat on the ground. When the shot had passed without hitting us we would get up and rush on the gun batteries like lightning so as to seize them before they had time to reload.

The Committee of Public Safety's response to this insubordination was swift and brutal. An army of 25,000 was sent

ENTER THE CORSICAN

The revolutionary government that followed the Reign of Terror, known as the Directory, was more moderate than the Jacobin-dominated National Assembly that had preceded

from Paris to pacify the region, destroying farms, villages, livestock, and crops. Almost half a million people may have died in the resulting famine. Here, revolutionary General Louis Marie Turreau writes to the minister of war boasting of his methods in the Vendée:

> My purpose is to burn everything. . . . All brigands caught bearing arms, or convicted of having taken up arms to revolt against their country, will be bayoneted. The same will apply to girls, women, and children in the same circumstances. Those who are merely under suspicion will not be spared either. . . . All villages, farms, woods, heathlands, generally anything which will burn, will be set on fire.

One enterprising revolutionary was commended in Paris because of the efficient way he disposed of large numbers of White suspects arriving in his city jail:

> An endless number of miscreants continues to arrive here. The guillotine is far too slow, and since shooting wastes powder and shot, it was decided to put a certain number of them in large boats, which are then taken to the middle of the river Loire, half a league from the town, and then sunk. This operation goes on constantly.*

* Richard Cobb and Colin Jones, eds. *The French Revolution: Voices from a Momentous Epoch 1789-1795* (London: Simon & Schuster, 1988).

A portrait of the French emperor Napoleon Bonaparte as king of Italy in 1805. The former artillery officer's ambitions enabled him to overthrow the French revolutionary government and become French emperor in 1804. Until his final defeat in 1815, he was master of much of Europe. The Napoleonic Code, the legal reforms he established at that time, remain influential in civil law jurisdictions around the globe.

it. The war with Austria, Britain, and many other European states, however, went on. In March 1796, the Directory sent an ambitious 26-year-old Corsican general, Napoleon Bonaparte, to take over the dilapidated French army fighting the Austrians in northern Italy. Much to their astonishment, not only did Napoleon defeat his enemies there, but also he sent his ragtag force all the way to the gates of Vienna, where the Austrian emperor hastily agreed to a peace treaty. Napoleon returned to France to be hailed as a hero.

Yet much to the Directory's misfortune, Bonaparte's ambitions were not restricted to military affairs. He desired political power too. Assisted by the equally talented and unscrupulous politician Charles Talleyrand, who would become his long-serving diplomatic adviser, Napoleon overthrew the Directory's leaders and installed himself as the head of a three-man Consulate government in 1799. Napoleon tolerated his two co-rulers for a few years before crowning himself emperor of France in 1804. According to legend, when Pope Pius VII, who was supposed to be leading the coronation ceremony, held out the imperial crown to Napoleon's head, the Corsican seized it and put it on himself.

Although today we tend to regard the French Revolution and the Napoleonic Wars as separate events, Europeans at the time thought of them as part of the same 25-year period of drama, triumph, and disaster. Napoleon, for all his splendid finery, always thought of himself as a good revolutionary who was simply continuing the principles of 1789 in a new, imperial style.

Between his coronation in 1804 and his downfall 10 years later after the Battle of Leipzig, Napoleon conquered most of continental Europe. He redrew and reorganized the map of Europe, which in some cases had remained the same since the Middle Ages, destroying ancient states and placing his brothers and sisters on the thrones of Spain, Holland, Italy, and Germany. He tore down political and legal systems that

(continues on page 28)

CHARLES MAURICE DE TALLEYRAND-PÉRIGORD (1754–1838)

The career of Charles Maurice de Talleyrand-Périgord, known to history simply as Charles Talleyrand, illustrates the shifting changes in fortunes that took place in France in the three decades following the revolution of 1789. The youth who trained to be a Catholic priest (though he was already an atheist) eventually became an ambassador for the French revolutionary republic; then grand chamberlain of the Napoleonic Empire; and finally, the chief negotiator for the restored House of Bourbon at the Congress of Vienna. Corrupt, cynical, and a notorious womanizer, Talleyrand owed his success to his diplomatic genius and his keen sense for knowing when it was time to shift allegiances. "Treason," he once said, "is a matter of dates." He for one always kept a careful eye on the calendar.

Talleyrand was born into an ancient and prestigious noble family, but a permanent limp in one of his legs left him unable to pursue an aristocratic career as a soldier and so he was ushered into the Church. After the fall of the Bastille, the revolutionary government sent him to Great Britain as an unofficial emissary. Talleyrand avoided the worst of the Reign of Terror by living in quasi-exile in England and the United States for several years. In 1796, he returned to France and was appointed foreign minister. After befriending the rising star General Bonaparte, Talleyrand took part in the 1799 coup d'état that made Napoleon first consul. He was rewarded with promotion and lavish personal gifts, but his diplomatic advice was often ignored, much to his frustration.

While today some regard Talleyrand as a master politician, others perceive him as an unprincipled opportunist who betrayed every government he worked for, including the Ancien Régime, the French Revolution, Napoleon, and the French Restoration.

In 1807, Talleyrand resigned his post as foreign minister. For the next seven years, he played an elaborate double game, apparently remaining the emperor's loyal ally while at the same time taking bribes from Napoleon's enemies and secretly advising Czar Alexander I. When the Sixth Coalition's forces entered Paris in 1814, Talleyrand had himself declared leader of the provisional government of France and offered his services to the newly restored king, Louis XVIII. At the Congress of Vienna, Talleyrand brilliantly exploited the tensions that existed between the members of the Sixth Coalition, and in doing so, was able to secure a lenient settlement for France. With the ending of the Congress, Talleyrand went into semiretirement for many years, though he continued to involve himself in shady political intrigues. In 1830, he served in one final post as King Louis-Philippe's ambassador to Great Britain.

(continued from page 25)

had existed for centuries and replaced them with constitutions and codes of his own. By the time of his surrender to the Sixth Coalition armies in April 1814, the Europe that had existed on the eve of the French Revolution had disappeared. It was up to the representatives of the Congress of Vienna to decide what could—and should—be restored.

Liberalism, Nationalism, and Conservatism

It was the people of Strasbourg, a town in eastern France, who first heard it. To begin with, it was just a distant hum, a wisp of a song in the distance. Then it grew louder, the words and tune slowly perceptible. "Arise children of the Fatherland," it went, "the day of glory has arrived!" And it continued:

> Against us tyranny's
> Bloody standard is raised
> Listen to the sound in the fields
> The howling of these fearsome soldiers
> They are coming into our midst
> To cut the throats of your sons and consorts
>
> To arms, citizens
> Form your battalions

March, march

Let impure blood

Water our furrows[1]

The song was being sung by troops from Marseilles, a city in southeastern France, who had arrived in Strasbourg on April 25, 1792, to defend the town against the counterrevolutionary armies of Austria. What they were performing was a ditty dreamed up by Rouget de Lisle, a military engineer, that he called "The War Song of the Army of the Rhine." The popularity of the song and its proud revolutionary lyrics spread across France within weeks, and de Lisle's creation—now renamed "La Marseillaise" in honor of its first singers—was soon the unofficial anthem of the French nation. A commentator for a French newspaper wrote: "They sing it very harmoniously, and when they get to the bit where they wave their hats and swords in the air and all shout together, *to arms, citizens!* it really sends a shiver down the spine."[2]

It certainly put a shiver down the spines of the crowned kings of Europe. The rousing popularity of "La Marseillaise" illustrated just how much the French Revolution was, by 1792, already becoming an ideological struggle—a battle for ideas— in which symbols and songs would be as powerful as muskets and cannons. Lazare Carnot, one of the dynamic reformers of the French Revolutionary armies, said that "La Marseillaise" was worth 100,000 soldiers, so effective was it in raising morale among the troops.

The revolutionaries were motivated by powerful new ideas—above all, the ideas of liberalism and nationalism. These ideas were to dominate the politics of Europe for more than a century after Napoleon's fall. Indeed, they were so prevailing that they inspired a counter-ideology, which came to be called conservatism. In fact, the basic terms that we today use in so much of modern political discussion—"left-wing," "right-wing," "radical," "reactionary"—were born in the aftermath of 1789, though they have often come to mean something quite different in twenty-first century America than they did in nineteenth-century Europe.

THE WORLD OF THE OLD ORDER

In order to better understand these ideas, it is important to get a sense of what Europe was like before the French Revolution and what the ideas of the "old order," as it became known, were.

Europe was then a continent of kings and emperors. The only republic on the continent was the tiny canton (or state) of Geneva in Switzerland, which was scarcely any bigger than the town itself. Otherwise, monarchs ruled, and they ruled absolutely. There were no restrictions on their power other than a few ancient rights held by the nobility and the Roman Catholic Church. Kings literally held the power of life and death over their subjects. In France, the Bourbon monarchs could issue *lettres de cachet*—special writs that allowed the authorities to imprison anyone without a trial or an appeal. Kings appointed ministers to manage the day-to-day business of state, but these ministers did not have to answer to a parliamentary body and held their positions purely at the behest of their monarchs. Government in Europe was *irresponsible*—not in the sense that it was foolish (though it often was) but in the sense that it could not be held responsible by any higher sovereign power. The rule of law as it exists in America and Europe today did not, in any practical sense, exist.

The only real exception to this was Great Britain, which, although it was a kingdom with a monarch, had a quite different system of responsible government, elected politicians, and legal restraints on royal authority. This would make Britain's ideological response to the French Revolution more complex than that of most other states.

A glance at a map will also show how different eighteenth-century Europe was from today. Germany and Italy did not exist as nations, but as abstract geographical entities. Germany was divided up into several hundred individual states, some of them (such as Bavaria and Saxony) quite large, but others so small that they could be ridden across in a matter of minutes. This was the Holy Roman Empire, a ramshackle collection of petty princedoms, duchies, and independent cities ruled in theory by the emperor of Austria, but in practice simply a patchwork carpet so flimsy that it was incapable of defending itself. Italy, though not quite so intricately split up, was nonetheless broken into about a dozen small and medium-sized states.

LIBERALISM: THE RIGHTS OF MAN

The origins of classical liberalism can probably be traced to the extraordinary intellectual movement of the eighteenth century known as the Enlightenment. During the Enlightenment, authors, artists, and philosophers across Europe began to discuss and write about the nature of existence in a new way. They rejected traditional and supernatural explanations of the human and physical worlds and insisted that intellectual reason was the only legitimate source of understanding and authority. In France especially, figures such as the writers Voltaire, Montesquieu, and Diderot became champions of free thought. They rejected appeals to custom and religious dogma as mere superstition.

Although the Enlightenment movement did not begin in an explicitly political way—if it was opposed to anything it was to the overarching power of the Catholic Church rather than the monarchs of Europe—the implications of its championing of reason soon became apparent. Why, after all, should kings rule absolutely over their subjects based on nothing more than centuries of tradition? Why should ordinary men, who were perfectly capable of intellectual thought, be held virtual slaves of monarchs simply on the grounds that it had always been so? Jean-Jacques Rousseau, a Swiss-born thinker, could see no justification for this. In his 1762 book *The Social Contract*, Rousseau argued that what he called the "general will" of the people was the only legitimate source of political authority;

kings governed on trust alone, and a monarch who abused his powers was a tyrant. "Man is born free," lamented Rousseau; "and everywhere he is in chains."[3] It was a message that was going to have explosive repercussions.

NATIONALISM: FOR LOVE OF COUNTRY

The basic demand of all nineteenth-century liberals was for their governments to have constitutions—written legal codes that enshrined the rights and, especially, the limits of state power over the citizen. From this, however, arose the question: What "natural" boundaries should the state have? This led to the other incendiary proposal of the age: the idea that the only legitimate state was a national one, made up of people with the same language, culture, and sense of ethnic identity.

The frontiers of eighteenth-century states observed no particular logical boundaries. The kingdom of France roughly corresponded to the geographical area in which most French-speakers lived, but other states were much more peculiar in shape. Prussia was a mixture of Poles and Germans. Russia was a multiethnic empire in which hundreds of languages were spoken. Austria was a jumble of Germans, Hungarians, and Slavs. Most of what is Germany today was broken up into the micro-states of the Holy Roman Empire. Italy, as Austrian Prince Klemens Wenzel von Metternich observed, was purely "a geographical expression."[4] Identities in places such as Italy and Germany were still largely defined in religious, local, and royal terms. That is to say, a farmer in eighteenth-century Carinthia probably regarded himself as a Christian, a Carinthian, and a subject of the emperor in Vienna rather than a German.

All this was to change with the French Revolution. With the execution of their king, the revolutionaries redefined their primary loyalty not to a man but to an idea: the idea of the French *patrie* (or "Fatherland") itself. It was for this cause that the men of Marseilles marched in 1792. The national idea was

(continues on page 36)

THE DECLARATION OF THE RIGHTS OF MAN AND OF THE CITIZEN (1789)

On August 26, 1789, France's National Assembly proclaimed a general statement summarizing the ideals of its recent revolt against royal despotism. The Declaration of the Rights of Man and of the Citizen became the preamble to the revolutionary constitution approved two years later. With its insistence on the sovereignty of the people, the Declaration was a stirring tribute to the principles of liberty, equality, and fraternity espoused by the revolutionaries of 1789. In practice, the Republican governments that followed the Declaration's adoption would choose to ignore its guarantees of a free press, a fair trial, and religious freedom. The liberal, romantic, and nationalist values that it encapsulated, however, would continue to inspire revolutionary dreamers long after the Bourbon kings had been restored to power in France.

In this excerpt, note the similarities and differences between the French Declaration and the U.S. Declaration of Independence drafted by Thomas Jefferson in 1776:

> Men are born and remain free and equal in rights. Social distinctions may be founded only upon the general good.
>
> The aim of all political association is the preservation of the natural and imprescriptible rights of man. These rights are liberty, property, security, and resistance to oppression.
>
> The principle of all sovereignty resides essentially in the nation. No body nor individual may exercise any authority which does not proceed directly from the nation.

Liberty consists in the freedom to do everything which injures no one else; hence the exercise of the natural rights of each man has no limits except those which assure to the other members of the society the enjoyment of the same rights. These limits can only be determined by law.

Law can only prohibit such actions as are hurtful to society. Nothing may be prevented which is not forbidden by law, and no one may be forced to do anything not provided for by law.

Law is the expression of the general will. Every citizen has a right to participate personally, or through his representative, in its foundation. It must be the same for all, whether it protects or punishes. All citizens, being equal in the eyes of the law, are equally eligible to all dignities and to all public positions and occupations, according to their abilities, and without distinction except that of their virtues and talents.

No person shall be accused, arrested, or imprisoned except in the cases and according to the forms prescribed by law. Any one soliciting, transmitting, executing, or causing to be executed, any arbitrary order, shall be punished. But any citizen summoned or arrested in virtue of the law shall submit without delay, as resistance constitutes an offense.

The law shall provide for such punishments only as are strictly and obviously necessary, and no one shall suffer punishment except it be legally inflicted in virtue of a law passed and promulgated before the commission of the offense.*

* "The Declaration of the Rights of Man and of the Citizen," The Avalon Project, Yale Law School. http://avalon.law.yale.edu/18th_century/rightsof.asp.

(continued from page 33)
to spread rapidly with the advance of the revolutionary armies. Indeed, it was in many places a response and a challenge to the French military conquests; by 1813, agitators in the Rhineland were recruiting their fellow countrymen to lead a war of liberation against Napoleon in the name of all the German people. The national idea was to prove infectious and volatile.

CONSERVATISM: TO PRESERVE AND IMPROVE

The initial response of the old regime's supporters to the events of 1789 was simply to condemn the revolutionaries as wicked and godless. It soon became clear, however, that the power of liberal and national ideology was simply too strong to ignore. Those who wanted to restore the status quo had to present intellectually respectable counterarguments. This forced them to go back to first principles and a build a logically coherent defense of their ideas. The result was the formation of conservatism, the first attempt to justify the absolute rule of kings by appealing to reason rather than simply tradition.

The British parliamentarian Edmund Burke developed what was probably the most influential conservative argument in his 1790 book *Reflections on the Revolution in France*. To Burke, the error of the Jacobins was that they had torn down the carefully constructed hierarchies and customs of their society, built up over centuries, without any clear idea of what they were going to erect in their place. The result, Burke argued, would be anarchy—a prediction that unsurprisingly gained force when the Reign of Terror broke out in France under Robespierre in 1792. Burke, like many other conservative thinkers, was not opposed to *any* change in society, but he thought reforms ought to be slow and incremental and guided by traditional institutions such as the monarchy and the aristocracy rather than the uneducated masses.

The French lawyer and diplomat Joseph de Maistre continued Burke's ideas in a series of books written in the early 1800s.

The British parliamentarian Edmund Burke, considered one of the founders of conservative thought for his opposition to the French Revolution, was also an advocate for liberal treatment of Britain's American colonies and supported the abolition of the Atlantic slave trade.

He placed particular emphasis on the role of the Church in a stable society; by worshipping reason alone rather than God, he argued, the revolutionaries had disrupted the divinely orga-

EDMUND BURKE (1729–1797)

On the face of it, Edmund Burke was an unlikely champion of the powers that be. A passionate critic of government policy in his native Britain, he spent much of his life supporting unpopular radical causes: He campaigned on behalf of votes for Catholics, criticized the East India Company for its treatment of South Asians, and defended the rebellious Americans during the Revolutionary War. Burke, however, was so alarmed by what he saw taking place in France in 1789 that he devoted the rest of his life to the ideological crusade against the Jacobins. He would go down in history as the first intellectual hero of what became known as conservatism.

Burke was born in Dublin, Ireland, the son of a successful lawyer. After attending Trinity College, he moved to London and joined the social circle of the influential statesman the Marquess of Rockingham, who eventually became British prime minister. Assisted by his high-ranking connections, Burke gained a seat in the House of Commons in 1765 and spent the next 30 years as a highly respected member of Parliament (MP). His seven-year campaign against the allegedly corrupt governor of the East India Company, Warren Hastings, led to major reforms in the way Britain governed its overseas empire.

Initially, Burke was undecided about the morality of the French Revolution. The turning point for him came

nized social contract. Indeed, the chaos that followed 1789 was, de Maistre contended, a divine punishment for the dangerous atheistic flirtations of the Enlightenment philosophers.

when a mob of Parisians attacked the royal family at their palatial home in Versailles in October 1789. Burke was so outraged at this assault on Louis XVI that he began writing a lengthy critique of the National Assembly and everything it stood for. Published the following year, Burke's book, *Reflections on the Revolution in France*, was an immediate publishing sensation, with 35,000 copies sold. At a time when many Britons were still sympathetic toward the revolutionaries, Burke was already warning that events in France would soon turn violent—a prediction that turned out to be eerily accurate.

Yet his book did far more than just criticize the Jacobins. Burke developed a sophisticated theory about the need to defend the traditional social order. He argued that society was a complex and fragile organism, the product of centuries of slow historical development, and that meddling with its ancient structure in the cause of abstract rights was more likely to cause misery than happiness. "What," wrote Burke, "is liberty without wisdom, and without virtue? It is the greatest of all possible evils; for it is folly, vice, and madness." At a time when the enemies of the French revolutionaries were on the defensive, Burke's book provided vital intellectual ammunition. Though the author of the *Reflections* was long dead by the time that the Congress of Vienna met in 1814, his ideas influenced the statesmen there. Austrian Prince Klemens Wenzel von Metternich and the other conservatives trying to restore the old European order were indebted to Burke's arguments.

Not surprisingly, perhaps, conservatism was most popular among those groups that had the most to lose from revolution, namely the nobility and the clergy. It never developed into a mass ideology in the same way that liberalism and nationalism did. Yet by developing a coherent response to the French Revolution rather than simply railing against it, writers such as Burke and de Maistre gave the conservative statesmen who met in Vienna in 1814 much greater confidence in trying to roll back the changes unleashed after the fall of the Bastille.

An Alliance of Rivals: The Great Powers in 1814

All the great powers that assembled in Vienna in 1814—Russia, Austria, Prussia, and Great Britain—sincerely wanted a future Europe of peace and security. Each nation, in its own way, had paid a high price to defeat Napoleon, and all the statesmen assembled in the Austrian capital wanted a period of stability to follow the rancorous quarter century of war and revolution they had just lived through. The problem, however, was that each power had a different idea about how this security ought to be achieved, and not all of them were compatible. The clashing goals of the Sixth Coalition members would greatly complicate the negotiations in Vienna and lead to inherent tension in the settlement that was eventually achieved.

The Congress of Vienna of 1814–1815 was not the first time that the great European powers sought to redraw the map of Europe in their favor. Seen here, a 1773 print shows European rulers discussing the first partition of Poland.

RUSSIA: THE GREAT EASTERN BEAR

Of all the great powers that met in Vienna in 1814, Russia arrived with perhaps the greatest moral authority of all. It was Russian soldiers who, in 1812, had battled Napoleon's army all the way from the burnt-out shell of Moscow westward across Europe. The Russians had constituted the greatest part of the army that defeated Bonaparte at Leipzig. Their stubborn resistance and their sacrifices had made the victory of the Sixth Coalition possible.

Yet Russia remained a mysterious, somewhat "foreign," country on the very fringe of Western civilization—in many ways a state that was as much Asian as it was European. Its people, though mostly Christian, worshipped in the Greek Orthodox tradition rather than the Catholic or Protestant ones, as the onion-shaped domes of their churches attested. To many congressional attendees, the Russians spoke a strange guttural language and dressed in peculiar clothes. The "uncouth" manners of the Russian representatives in Vienna were soon to become one of the scandals of the Congress. Russia's czar, Alexander I, was as eccentric as the country he led; his father, Paul, who was probably insane, had been murdered by his own noblemen. These were not the hallmarks of a "civilized" society. So Alexander's million-strong army aroused as much fear and suspicion as it did admiration. The European imagination had been haunted for centuries by the specter of hordes of barbarians riding from the east. Now that the defeat of Napoleon had whetted their appetite, would the Russians be content to leave the rest of the continent in peace?

Of course, much of this was just snobbery and prejudice. Alexander, a deeply religious man who had been horrified by the bloodshed of the revolutionary years, had no intention of continuing the war. Like all Russians, however, he was seeking a prize for his country's victory. The prize he had in mind most of all was Poland.

Poland had been a powerful independent state in the Middle Ages, but by the eighteenth century it was proving

At the time of the Congress of Vienna, Czar Alexander I of Russia was seen as a hero to many Europeans for defeating Napoleon. This 1814 print shows an idealized version of the monarch bringing peace to Europe.

too ramshackle to protect itself from its ambitious neighbors to the east, west, and south. In a series of mutually agreed upon carve-ups, the Russians, Prussians, and Austrians had partitioned the kingdom among themselves. When Napoleon conquered Prussia in 1806, he had resurrected the Polish state, calling it the Grand Duchy of Warsaw, and Polish troops had fought for Bonaparte throughout the rest of the war. Poland, in fact, had been the springboard for the invasion of Russia in 1812. Now the Russians wanted to swallow up as much of Poland as they could, if possible annexing Prussia and Austria's old portions too.

If this seemed like aggression, Alexander could make the reasonable argument that Russia was merely securing its western frontier with a buffer zone. The Russians had, after all, just seen their country plundered and their biggest city burnt to the ground. With that in mind, asking for an extra layer of defense did not seem quite so outrageous. Whether the Poles themselves were keen on the idea was another matter, of course.

AUSTRIA: "A WORM-EATEN HOUSE"

The Austrian Empire lay at the heart of central Europe. One of the oldest states on the continent, its rulers had been the first of the continental monarchies to confront the Jacobin revolutionaries. Austria was tough. Defeated multiple times by Napoleon, including most spectacularly at the Battle of Austerlitz in 1805, it had nonetheless rebounded and eventually became one of the key members of the victorious Sixth Coalition. The Austrians could take some pride in their sheer ability to survive no end of misfortunes.

Of all the states of Europe, however, Austria had perhaps the most to fear from the French Revolution. The empire's boundaries were large, but made no logical sense. Having accumulated bits and pieces of territory over the centuries, Austria's rulers led a polyglot collection of subjects of many different languages and cultures: Germans, Hungarians, Czechs, Italians, Croats, Poles, and Slovaks, to name just a few. It did not take much imagination to see what chaos an ideology such as nationalism would

PRINCE KLEMENS WENZEL VON METTERNICH (1773-1859)

Few statesmen in history have been as successful and as pessimistic as Prince von Metternich. For almost 40 years, he directed the foreign policy of one of the great powers of Europe and played a key role in the negotiations at the Congress of Vienna. Yet toward the end of his career, Metternich was haunted by the conviction that all his work had been fruitless. Certainly his attempt to prevent the spread of liberal and national ideas in Germany and Italy proved ineffective. Metternich's diplomatic skills, however, were unsurpassed in his lifetime, and as "coachman of Europe," as he was known by many of his contemporaries, he shaped the political destiny of the continent for more than a century.

Metternich was born in Koblenz, the son of a minor German nobleman of the Holy Roman Empire who had served as Austria's ambassador to the Rhineland. As a boy, he spent his youth traipsing around the diplomatic courts of the old regime. In 1788, Metternich went to university in Strasbourg, but the outbreak of the French Revolution the following year interrupted his studies, and he followed his father's career by joining the Austrian diplomatic corps. A posting to Prussia in 1803 proved so successful that Napoleon personally requested that Metternich be sent to represent Austria in Paris. When Austria resumed

bring to this clutter of peoples. If all the ethnic groups within the Austrian Empire demanded national rights to popular self-determination, the whole edifice would crumble. No wonder

war against France in 1809, Metternich was returned to Vienna under armed guard. Upon arrival, he was made Emperor Francis I's foreign minister, a post he would hold until 1848.

Austria's attack on the French Empire turned to disaster. Under the harsh terms of the peace treaty, it was forced to hand over considerable territory to France. Metternich, who felt that appeasing Napoleon was the best policy for Austria to pursue until it gathered its strength again, negotiated a marriage between the Corsican and Francis I's daughter Marie-Louise. In 1812, when France invaded Russia, Metternich even agreed to provide some Austrian troops in support. He was, however, already in secret negotiations with Czar Alexander I, and when the French army was destroyed on the retreat from Moscow, Austria switched sides. In recognition of his services, Metternich was made a prince of Austria in 1813.

After his success at the postwar Congress of Vienna, Metternich spent the next 30 years attempting to maintain a stable conservative equilibrium in central Europe. He maintained a close watch on liberals and nationalists through a vast and efficient network of spies, informers, and secret police that operated according to his bidding. Not surprisingly, this made Metternich one of the most hated as well as feared men alive. When revolution finally broke out in Vienna in 1848, an angry mob gathered at his office door to demand his resignation. After a brief exile in England, Metternich returned to Austria in 1851, but his career was over. He died eight years later.

that Austria's foreign minister, Prince von Metternich (who admitted in private that his empire was "a worm-eaten house") was so determined to strangle liberal and national sentiments.

Austria had been required to hand over a lot of territory during the Napoleonic Wars, but Metternich did not necessarily want it all back. The Austrian Netherlands, for instance, separated from the rest of the empire by hundreds of miles, had always been more of a liability than an asset. Nor was Metternich interested in restoring the Holy Roman Empire, which the emperors of Austria had ruled (though in name only) for centuries. In 1806, Napoleon had dissolved it and replaced it with something called the Confederation of the Rhine, which had roughly the same frontiers but was made up of a much smaller number of medium-sized states. This actually made a lot more sense than the Holy Roman Empire had ever made, and Metternich was content to leave Napoleon's reforms in place with only some minor adjustments.

The big changes that Metternich wanted to see lay in Italy. The Austrian foreign minister was worried that Russia and Prussia would emerge too strong from the Congress of Vienna, and so he wanted his empire to annex large portions of northern Italy so as to counterbalance its northern and eastern neighbors. Like the other representatives of the great powers in 1814, Metternich could justify his ambitions on the grounds of security. If Austria, Prussia, and Russia were kept in rough balance, or equilibrium, war between any two of them was less likely. By acquiring new Italian territory, however, Metternich would be making the empire even more multinational than it already was. He would be storing up all kinds of troubles for himself and his successors.

PRUSSIA: "AN ARMY WITH A STATE ATTACHED"

Prussia was the smallest and newest of all the great powers that met in Vienna in 1814, as it had become a kingdom only in 1701. It straddled the Baltic coast of Germany from Brandenburg in the west to Konigsberg in the east, a sparsely populated and rather agriculturally barren swath of land. Throughout their history, the Prussians had been surrounded by hostile neighbors and had had to fight hard to avoid extinction, leaving the country's army its only really strong and reliable institution. The joke was that instead of being a state that happened to have an army, Prussia was an army with a state attached. In 1814, few people would have guessed that half a century later Prussia would evolve to become the heart of the most powerful empire in Europe.

After defeating the Prussians in 1806, Napoleon had imposed a harsh peace treaty on their king, Frederick William III, seizing almost half the kingdom's territory. At the Congress of Vienna, the Prussian delegation wanted these lands returned but also sought additional compensation elsewhere. Prussia was not interested in more Polish territory—there were already too many Poles in the kingdom for the country's comfort—but it did want to annex some of the more attractive minor German states of Napoleon's Confederation of the Rhine.

The single most valuable target was Saxony, which lay on Prussia's southwestern border. The Saxons were old enemies of the Prussians. As Napoleon's allies, they had proved to be a bit too enthusiastic for their own good. The Congress seemed like a perfect opportunity to expand the Prussian frontier and eliminate a longstanding and dangerous rival. The Prussian delegation, however, was also keenly aware that it had the least diplomatic influence of all the great powers meeting in Vienna. So to some extent, King Frederick William III would have to be happy with what he got.

GREAT BRITAIN: BRITANNIA RULES THE WAVES

Britain's position at the Congress of Vienna was different from that of all the other great powers. As an island nation, it was not interested in acquiring any land for itself on the European

(continues on page 53)

KING FREDERICK WILLIAM III'S PROCLAMATION TO THE PRUSSIAN PEOPLE (1813)

The crowned kings and emperors who fought Bonaparte in the last years of the Napoleonic Wars faced a dilemma. They needed to inspire their subjects to march against the French army, and there was no better way to do this than the rhetoric of patriotic nationalism—but national feeling, inspired by the French Revolution, was just the kind of radical ideology they were fighting to suppress. A proclamation by King Frederick William III of Prussia to his "loyal subjects" in 1813 contained just this kind of tension. The king appealed, successfully, to his people's sense of German nationhood. Would he be able to control their patriotic emotions once Napoleon was gone? That was as yet unclear. The following is an excerpt from his proclamation:

> There is no need of explaining to my loyal subjects, or to any German, the reasons for the war which is about to begin. They lie plainly before the eyes of awakened Europe. We succumbed to the superior force of France. The peace which followed deprived me of my people and, far from bringing us blessings, it inflicted upon us deeper wounds than the war itself, sucking out the very marrow of the country. . . . The purest and best of intentions on my part were of no avail against insolence and faithlessness, and it became only too plain that Napoleon's treaties would gradually ruin us even more surely than his wars. The moment is come when we can no longer harbor the slightest illusion as to our situation.
>
> Brandenburgers, Prussians, Silesians, Pomeranians, Lithuanians! You know what you have borne for the past

seven years; you know the sad fate that awaits you
if we do not bring this war to an honorable end. . . .
Remember the blessings for which your forefathers
fought under their leadership and which they paid for
with their blood—freedom of conscience, national honor,
independence, commerce, industry, learning. Look at
the great example of our powerful allies, the Russians;
look at the Spaniards, the Portuguese. For such objects
as these even weaker peoples have gone forth against
mightier enemies and returned in triumph. Witness the
heroic Swiss and the people of the Netherlands.

Great sacrifices will be demanded from every class
of the people, for our undertaking is a great one, and
the number and resources of our enemies far from
insignificant. But would you not rather make these sacrifices for the Fatherland and for your own rightful king
than for a foreign ruler, who, as he has shown by many
examples, will use you and your sons and your utter-
most farthing for ends which are nothing to you?

Faith in God, perseverance, and the powerful aid
of our allies will bring us victory as the reward of our
honest efforts. Whatever sacrifices may be required
of us as individuals, they will be outweighed by the
sacred rights for which we make them, and for which
we must fight to a victorious end unless we are will-
ing to cease to be Prussians or Germans. This is the
final, the decisive struggle; upon it depends our independence, our prosperity, our existence. There are no
other alternatives but an honorable peace or a heroic
end. You would willingly face even the latter for
honor's sake, for without honor no Prussian or German
could live.*

---

* Frederick William III, "Proclamation Of Frederick William
of Prussia to His People," March 17, 1813. From *Readings in
Modern European History*, eds. James Harvey Robinson and
Charles A. Beard (Boston: Ginn, 1908), pp. 363-365.

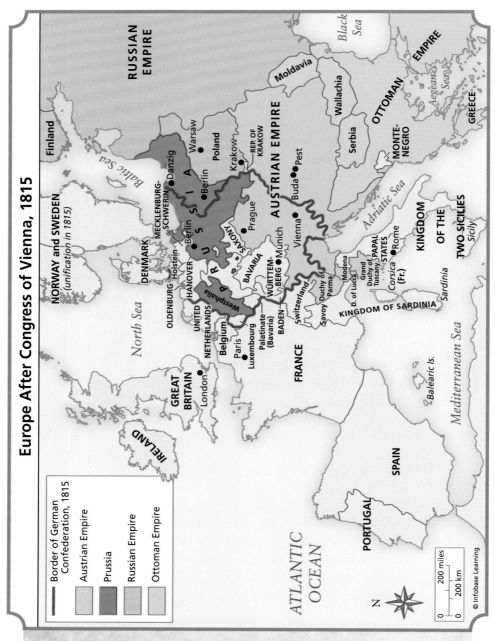

Europe After Congress of Vienna, 1815

RUSSIAN EMPIRE

Finland

Baltic Sea

NORWAY and SWEDEN
(unification in 1815)

North Sea

DENMARK

MECKLENBURG-SCHWERIN

Danzig

Warsaw •

Poland

REP. OF KRAKOW

Krakow •

Berlin •

P R U S S I A

Berlin •

SAXONY

Prague •

Moldavia

Wallachia

Serbia

OTTOMAN EMPIRE

Black Sea

Aegean Sea

GREECE

MONTE-NEGRO

AUSTRIAN EMPIRE

Buda •• Pest

Vienna •

Munich •

Holstein •

HANOVER

OLDENBURG

Westphalia

UNITED NETHERLANDS

Belgium

Paris •

Luxembourg

Palatinate (Bavaria)

BAVARIA

WÜRTEM-BERG

BADEN

Switzerland

Savoy

Grand Duchy of Parma

D. of Lucca

Modena

Grand Duchy of Tuscany

PAPAL STATES

Rome •

Corsica (Fr.)

Adriatic Sea

KINGDOM OF THE TWO SICILIES

Sicily

Sardinia

KINGDOM OF SARDINIA

FRANCE

GREAT BRITAIN

London •

IRELAND

ATLANTIC OCEAN

PORTUGAL

SPAIN

Balearic Is.

Mediterranean Sea

Legend:
— Border of German Confederation, 1815
Austrian Empire
Prussia
Russian Empire
Ottoman Empire

N

200 miles
200 km
0
0

© Infobase Learning

This political map shows the national boundaries of Europe after the Congress of Vienna, which tried to reestablished the pre-revolutionary balance of power on the continent.

(continued from page 49)

continent. During the Napoleonic Wars, Britain had conquered most of the French and Dutch overseas colonial empires, including territories such as Malta, Ceylon (now Sri Lanka), and South Africa, and all it wanted the Congress to do was to ratify these annexations. Since the Royal Navy had dominated the world's sea lanes since smashing the French and Spanish fleets at the Battle of Trafalgar in 1805, there was little in practice that the other members of the Sixth Coalition could have done about this even if they had wanted to. So in that sense, securing Britain's goals in Vienna was going to be relatively easy for its foreign secretary, Lord Castlereagh.

The British, however, were extremely concerned that certain parts of the former Napoleonic Empire in Europe could potentially end up in hostile hands. Their greatest anxiety was over the fate of the Austrian Netherlands, which stood on the opposite side of the English Channel from Britain. This territory (roughly corresponding to modern-day Belgium) was not very large, but it included key port cities such as Antwerp. Britain's fear was that if an aggressive power used the shipbuilding yards of Antwerp to construct a fleet, it could challenge the Royal Navy's control of the North Sea, and hence threaten invasion. Clearly, extracting the Austrian Netherlands from French control was a British priority. The Austrians, however, who had other problems to worry about, were not interested in resuming their occupation. Britain did not want to annex the territory itself; so to whom should it be trusted?

The British had a complicated attitude towards the other powers' conservatism and antinationalism. On the one hand, they had deplored the violent excesses of the French Revolution, such as the murder of Louis XVI, and sought above all peace and tranquility on the European continent, which the liberal and national movements were likely to disrupt. On the other hand, the British state was itself fairly liberal. It was the only great power that had a constitution in 1814, and its government was run by a parliament elected by the wealthier members of the population. Though it was hardly a model democracy by today's standards, Britain was nonetheless the most representative and least repressive state in Europe. Because many of its people openly sympathized with the continental liberals and nationalists, the British government could not ignore public opinion. So Lord Castlereagh was suspicious of any attempts by Metternich to use the Congress as way of crushing the spread of free ideas. Though the delegates tried to brush it off at the meeting itself, this underlying ideological tension would eventually lead to the break-up of the Congress System.

The Congress Convenes

On October 1, 1814, the first session of the Congress of Vienna was formally held. The Austrian capital was abuzz with activity. Representatives from more than 200 governments were in attendance, though it soon became clear that the really important decisions were going to be made by the four biggest powers of the Sixth Coalition: Russia, Prussia, Austria, and Great Britain. The smaller states of Europe were to be spectators, not active participants.

For the rest of the delegates, however, Vienna held plenty of distractions that fall. Emperor Francis I had spent the enormous sum of 30 million florins to provide entertainment for his thousands of assembled guests, be they statesmen, soldiers, society ladies, servants, officials, or other hangers-on. Each night there was an elaborate evening banquet in the emperor's

Hofburg Palace, with dinner set for 40 tables. There were balls, receptions, tournaments, excursions to the countryside, and hot-air balloon displays. Even the most important guests could not wholly avoid the social whirl. Lord Castlereagh, a notoriously poor dancer, had to take lessons while in Vienna in order to avoid embarrassment.

THE FIRST TREATY OF PARIS

Long before members of the Sixth Coalition met in session in Vienna, the most urgent problem that it had to address in the spring of 1814 was what to do with its defeated enemy, France, and more specifically Napoleon Bonaparte, who, after abdicating the throne in April, had retired to a palace in Fontainebleau, south of Paris, to await his fate.

Two of the most important decisions were taken by Czar Alexander I alone, because he was the first of the Sixth Coalition leaders to reach the French capital. After arriving in Paris with his army, Alexander immediately sent for Charles Talleyrand, Napoleon's former foreign minister, and asked for his advice concerning the future of France. Talleyrand, who was never slow to seize an opportunity, recommended that Louis XVI's brother, who had been living in exile ever since the outbreak of the French Revolution, should be invited to return to the throne. A restoration of the Bourbon dynasty was not necessarily the first choice of all the other allies—the Austrians, for instance, would have preferred to have Napoleon's second wife, Marie-Louise, the daughter of their emperor, to rule instead. Before they had time to do anything about it, Louis was in Paris, declaring himself King Louis XVIII (not Louis XVII, out of respect for his brother's young son, who had died years earlier while being held prisoner by the Jacobins).

As for Napoleon, Alexander decided to be lenient. He allowed the Corsican to keep his title, awarded him a pension, and sent him off to be governor of the Mediterranean island of

Not all of the Congress of Vienna was serious business. Many entertainments were to be had by the delegates, including this ball in the Redoutensaal, which included a performance of Beethoven's Seventh Symphony and his composition *Wellington's Victory, or, the Battle of Vitoria.*

Elba. When Prince von Metternich and Castlereagh heard of this, they were uneasy. Elba, only a short distance from France, gave Napoleon opportunity to continue making mischief. As it turned out, their concern would be well founded. Within a year, Bonaparte would be back in France leading a new army against the forces of the coalition.

What, however, of France? The coalition leaders had every reason to impose a harsh settlement on the helpless country that had caused them so much trouble. Here, Talleyrand proved his worth to King Louis XVIII. The French foreign minister argued that it was neither moral nor sensible for the Sixth Coalition to

(continues on page 60)

CZAR ALEXANDER I (1777–1825)

Czar Alexander I's political life began and ended in intrigue. He became ruler of Russia when his father was deposed and murdered, his personal role in the coup d'etat forever remaining murky. After his funeral in 1825, persistent rumors spread that he had faked his own death and was living as a hermit or a monk in a remote monastery. These mysteries reflected Alexander's own enigmatic character. Unpredictable, paranoiac, and deeply spiritual, his diplomatic aims shifted between the pragmatic interests of his empire and his mystical belief in a union among all Christian monarchs.

His grandmother, Empress Catherine the Great, raised Alexander, and it is possible that she planned to pass the imperial crown directly to him rather than to his questionably sane father, Paul. In 1796, however, Catherine died without having taken the necessary legal steps, and Paul succeeded to the throne. Five years later, a group of court conspirators, dissatisfied by Paul's eccentric rule, burst into the emperor's bedroom one evening and strangled him to death. Historians have suggested that Alexander was complicit in the coup, but he believed his father would be allowed to abdicate unharmed. If that was the case, Paul's murder must have shaken the young Alexander. Certainly he was gripped by bouts of remorse and suspicion in his later life.

Alexander began his rule hoping to enact various liberal reforms throughout his autocratic empire, but his attention was soon drawn to international matters because of the rise of Napoleon Bonaparte. In December 1805, he was personally present on the battlefield at Austerlitz when the Russian Army was smashed, along with its Austrian ally, by Napoleon's forces. Alexander continued to fight Bonaparte for another two years, but after a series of further defeats in 1807, he agreed to sue for peace, and famously negotiated with the French emperor on a raft floating in the middle of the river Niemen in Poland. The Treaty of Tilsit, as it became known, lasted for five years until Napoleon, frustrated at Alexander's unwillingness to boycott British trade, invaded Russia with half a million troops. After the campaign ended in disaster for the French, Alexander triumphantly led his army across Europe, reaching Paris in the spring of 1814. It was he who personally organized the restoration of the Bourbon king, Louis XVIII, to the French throne and sent Napoleon to his brief exile on the Mediterranean island of Elba.

The size and power of the Russian empire meant that Alexander was a force to be reckoned with at the Congress of Vienna, but his peculiar and erratic behavior left other statesmen puzzled. Many wondered whether he was afflicted with the same insanity as his father. While his invitation to Europe's kings to create a permanent Holy Alliance at the end of the Congress was apparently sincere, the anti-liberal Prince von Metternich, who during the next five years gained a powerful influence over the impressionable Alexander, cynically exploited it. As he entered old age, Alexander abandoned his youthful attempts at reform at home and became increasingly despotic.

In 1825, he died suddenly from typhoid while traveling in the south of Russia. Over the years that followed, however, conspiracy theories grew that Alexander was secretly still alive. Remarkably, on the anniversary of his death in 1925, his tomb was opened and found to be empty.

(continued from page 57)
treat France severely. The House of Bourbon was not to blame for the actions of the revolutionaries or of Napoleon, so on what grounds could the allies punish Louis XVIII? In any case, the balance of power in Europe depended on the continued existence of a strong French state. If France were made too weak, it would create a power vacuum in Western Europe that would destabilize the delicate equilibrium between all the great powers.

Talleyrand's logic overcame the skepticism of the coalition statesmen. On May 20, 1814, the First Treaty of Paris was signed. France had to give up a modest amount of land on its eastern borders and renounce any territorial claims on its neighbors. Other than that, however, there was to be no punishment. The French did not have to pay any compensation to their former enemies. King Louis could maintain an army. He was even allowed to keep the art treasures that Napoleon had looted. It was a remarkable first victory for Talleyrand, one of many that were to follow at the Congress of Vienna itself.

THE POLISH QUESTION

As far back as February 1813, the Prussian king Frederick-William III and Russia's Alexander I had been thinking about the postwar future of Poland. When they signed their treaty of alliance in the Polish town of Kalisch, bringing Prussia into the war against Napoleon, they included a secret protocol in which they agreed to share some of the territorial spoils of the war between themselves. Russia was to get all of Poland, including the territories previously held by Prussia (known as Posen) and Austria (Galicia), while as compensation Prussia would be allowed to annex the whole of the Kingdom of Saxony.

The other Sixth Coalition powers were not told of this agreement during the war itself. When the complete details of the Treaty of Kalisch emerged at the Congress of Vienna, they were furious. Metternich seethed at the thought of having to give up Galicia and feared that Prussia would emerge from

Seen here, an 1815 caricature of Talleyrand, with a devil whispering in his ear. Talleyrand's successes at the Congress of Vienna were a testament to his political skills as well as to his machinations.

the Congress too powerful after swallowing up all of Saxony. Britain's Lord Castlereagh was also agitated; this secret deal went completely against the supposedly open and friendly spirit of the Congress. The two sides appeared deadlocked, with Prussia and Russia insisting that Kalisch should be honored, and Britain and Austria equally determined to foil it. The argument became so heated at one point that Alexander challenged Metternich to a duel and was talked out of it only through the personal intervention of Emperor Francis I of Austria.

Talleyrand saw another opening for himself. He approached Metternich and Castlereagh and offered France's support in the squabble with the Prussians and Russians. In January 1815, the three signed a secret pact pledging to support one another in case the disagreement turned to war. It was a remarkable turnaround; less than a year after Napoleon had abdicated, France's oldest rivals were asking for its support in a possible conflict with their own allies. In the end, Alexander and Frederick-William backed down. The result was a compromise: Russia got to annex most of Poland, but not Posen or Galicia; the Prussians were allowed to take just half of Saxony. The biggest winner of all was France—Talleyrand's brilliant exploitation of the quarrel enabled him to promote his country as a full equal of the other Congress powers. Louis's minister could not help but exult in his success. He was, as he wrote confidentially to a friend, contemptuous of the allied statesmen in Vienna. They were, he boasted, "too frightened to fight each other," yet also "too stupid to agree."[1]

GERMANY, ITALY, AND THE LOW COUNTRIES

In theory, the Sixth Coalition partners were committed to the principle of legitimacy—the idea that all of the traditional rulers of Europe who had been deposed from their thrones by the French revolutionaries or by Napoleon ought to be restored to their rightful territories. In practice, however, the Congress's statesmen recognized legitimacy when it suited them and ignored it when it did not. Europe was reorganized according to the interests and wishes of the five great powers (which now included France again), and if a legitimate monarch was an inconvenience, then it was too bad for him.

The clearest examples of this can be seen in the Congress's treatment of Germany and Italy. All the great powers agreed that it was impractical to restore the Holy Roman Empire with its hundreds of tiny statelets, and so a slightly modified form of Napoleon's Confederation of the Rhine, now simply called the German Confederation, was organized. There were 37 members of the confederation, which were to send representatives to a diet, or parliament, in Frankfurt. Austria and Prussia were also represented in the Confederation Diet. The Confederation certainly did not amount to a unified German state, which Metternich would never have allowed, but its medium-sized states were large enough to defend themselves rather better than the Holy Roman Empire had ever been.

Austria and Prussia were awarded territory too. Metternich took control of most of northern Italy, including Milan and Venice, and placed relatives of the Austrian emperor on some of the other Italian thrones (including Napoleon's second wife, Marie-Louise, who was granted the Duchy of Parma). Prussia, smarting from its loss of half of Saxony, had to make do with the Rhineland in western Germany. At the time this seemed like a poor deal for the Prussians. The region, however, would transform the European balance of power later in the nineteenth century when the Rhineland would become the greatest industrial center on the continent. No one could have predicted that in 1814.

As for the former Austrian Netherlands, these were handed over to the king of Holland. The British were highly satisfied with this deal. Holland was neutral and so presented no threat to the supremacy of the Royal Navy. The people of the Austrian Netherlands themselves were far less happy about the arrangement; being mostly Catholic, they objected to being placed under the rule of a Protestant monarch. Neither Castlereagh nor anyone else had consulted them, however, and their views were not solicited at the Congress. As it turned out, the union was to be a short-lived one.

By the end of March 1815, the statesmen in Vienna had every reason to be pleased. Although the five months of the Congress so far had not been short of acrimony, all of the great powers had been able to overcome their differences and reach a settlement which, if not ideal, was at least reasonably acceptable. Then, however, a message suddenly arrived from

(continues on page 66)

METTERNICH'S *POLITICAL CONFESSION OF FAITH* (1820)

Prince Klemens Wenzel von Metternich was convinced that the bloody turmoil of the French Revolution and Napoleonic era would be reproduced again unless Europe's monarchs agreed to stamp out all signs of liberal and nationalist sentiments among their subjects. In his *Political Confession of Faith*, Metternich laid out the philosophical justification for his conservative views:

> The revolutionary seed [has] penetrated into every country. . . . We are convinced that society can no longer be saved without strong and vigorous resolutions on the part of the Governments still free in their opinions and actions. We are also convinced that this may yet be, if the Governments face the truth, if they free themselves from all illusion, if they join their ranks and take their stand on a line of correct, unambiguous, and frankly announced principles.
>
> By this course the monarchs will fulfill the duties imposed upon them by Him who, by entrusting them with power, has charged them to watch over the maintenance of justice, and the rights of all, to avoid the paths of error, and tread firmly in the way of truth. Placed beyond the passions which agitate society, it is in days of trial chiefly that they are called upon to despoil realities of their false appearances, and to show themselves as they are, fathers invested with the authority belonging by right to the heads of families, to prove that, in days of mourning, they know how to be just, wise, and there-

fore strong, and that they will not abandon the people whom they ought to govern to be the sport of factions, to error and its consequences, which must involve the loss of society. . . .

The first principle to be followed by the monarchs, united as they are by the coincidence of their desires and opinions, should be that of maintaining the stability of political institutions against the disorganized excitement which has taken possession of men's minds—the immutability of principles against the madness of their interpretation; and respect for laws actually in force against a desire for their destruction. . . .

Let them be just, but strong; beneficent, but strict.

Let them maintain religious principles in all their purity, and not allow the faith to be attacked and morality interpreted according to the *social contract* or the visions of foolish sectarians.

Let them suppress Secret Societies, that gangrene of society.

In short, let the great monarchs strengthen their union, and prove to the world that if it exists, it is beneficent, and ensures the political peace of Europe: that it is powerful only for the maintenance of tranquility at a time when so many attacks are directed against it; that the principles which they profess are paternal and protective, menacing only the disturbers of public tranquility. . . .

To every great State determined to survive the storm there still remain many chances of salvation, and a strong union between the States on the principles we have announced will overcome the storm itself.*

---

* Klemens Wenzel, Prince von Metternich, *Memoirs of Prince Metternich* (New York: H. Fertig, 1970).

(continued from page 63)
Paris that shook the confidence of the delegates to the core. Napoleon Bonaparte had landed in southern France and was marching on the capital with a growing retinue of armed followers. The Corsican ogre they thought they had banished for good was back. "A thousand candles," wrote one courtier who was present when the news arrived, "seemed snuffed out in a second."[2]

Napoleon Returns: The Hundred Days

The small, balding man, wrapped in his long, gray army coat, stood before the ranks of trembling musketeers. It was the morning of March 7, 1815, near the village of Laffrey, south of Grenoble in the mountainous southeast of France. Napoleon Bonaparte, with a few hundred dedicated bodyguards, had slipped away from Elba a week before and landed in secret on France's Mediterranean shoreline. A battalion of a thousand soldiers of the 5th Infantry Regiment had been dispatched to intercept and arrest Bonaparte as he and his small entourage marched toward Paris. Now, at Laffrey, they stood within pistol range of one another. Napoleon, showing great calm and self-confidence, walked alone toward the infantrymen barring his way, their guns pointed directly at his chest. "Soldiers of the 5th Regiment!" the Corsican cried out. "If there is a single one of you who wants to kill his Emperor, here I am!"[1]

This painting depicts the euphoria that gripped French soldiers as they carried Napoleon into the Tuileries Palace in March 1815. The Congress of Vienna responded to Napoleon's return from exile by branding him an outlaw and vowing to defeat him once again.

Napoleon's audacious gamble paid off. The men of the 5th broke ranks and embraced their beloved emperor. Over the next 10 days, opposition to Bonaparte melted away across France as more and more of his veteran soldiers abandoned their recent oaths of loyalty to Louis XVIII and returned to the side of the man who had led them to such glory. By March 19, Napoleon was in Paris, cheered on by crowds of hysterical supporters. There was no one there to overthrow; after the news of what happened at Laffrey, Louis XVIII had fled to the Austrian Netherlands.

During the next three and a half months, a period that would go down in history as the Hundred Days, Napoleon briefly reemerged as leader of one of the great powers of Europe. His dramatic return threatened to undo everything that had been agreed at the Congress of Vienna. To the leaders of the Sixth Coalition, the prompt removal of this international menace assumed the highest priority. Who, however, would be up to the challenge of defeating the man who had once held the continent in his iron grip?

NAPOLEON OUTLAWED

Once reinstalled in Paris, Napoleon immediately wrote to Czar Alexander, Emperor Francis, and the other Allied leaders, insisting that he had no intention of restarting the war. His only desire, he said, was to reassume the peaceful rule of France itself. Whether this was actually true will never be known, because the decision had already been taken out of his hands.

Back in Vienna, Talleyrand had been working fast. When he heard of Napoleon's escape from Elba, the French delegate was horrified. He knew that the return of his old protégé would wreck all the careful work he had done on France's behalf at the Congress. So Talleyrand immediately lobbied to have Napoleon personally, rather than France, made the target of the Sixth Coalition's wrath. The Congress published a statement (drafted by Talleyrand) declaring the great leader a "wild beast" and a "bandit" who had lost "his sole lawful right to exist." "Napoleon Bonaparte," it went on, "has placed himself outside all human relations and . . . as the enemy and disturber of the peace of the world, he has delivered himself up to public justice."[2] In effect, it was saying that Napoleon could be killed by any man with impunity.

Of course, no one believed that Bonaparte would give up without a fight. He remained enormously popular in France and was already raising an army to defend himself. His military genius remained unsurpassed. After agreeing to each raise 150,000 troops to suppress Napoleon's coup, the Russian, Prussian, Austrian, and British delegations met to decide on a strategy. It would take time for the Russian and Austrian armies to mobilize and march on Paris, and it was expected that Napoleon would take the initiative and try to knock out some

ARTHUR WELLESLEY, 1ST DUKE OF WELLINGTON (1769–1852)

One of the greatest leaders of the Napoleonic Wars, Arthur Wellesley, honored as the duke of Wellington by the grateful British nation in 1814, capped his military career by defeating Napoleon decisively at the Battle of Waterloo the following year. He went on to represent his country throughout most of the Congress of Vienna and ultimately served twice as prime minister. Emotionally reserved and aloof, Wellington lived as a simple soldier throughout his life, even sleeping on a plain camp bed. Yet he showed an unusual concern for the well-being of his men and earned their fierce loyalty and devotion as a result.

Wellington was born in his family's townhouse in Dublin, Ireland. His father, the earl of Mornington, owned country estates in Ireland, but as the family's fourth son, young Arthur stood to inherit no property and so needed to choose a career instead. He joined the British Army in 1787 and also served as a member of Ireland's House of Commons. After military service in the Austrian Netherlands (today's Belgium), he was sent to India in 1797, where his brother was governor-general. During his eight years in India, Wellington became famous for his successful campaigns against the enemies of the British East India Company and amassed a considerable fortune in loot captured from his enemies. In 1805, tired of the tropical climate, he requestof his opponents one by one before he was overwhelmed. So the first line of defense would fall to the British and the Prussians, who had the nearest available troops. Marshal Gerhard von

ed a transfer back to Europe. In 1807, after a short interlude in which he served as the government's chief secretary for Ireland, Wellington was asked to assist Britain's ally Portugal, which was fighting against Napoleon's forces.

Wellington not only successfully defended the Portuguese capital of Lisbon using a brilliantly conceived line of fortifications, but in 1809 he went on the offensive with his small but well-trained and equipped Anglo-Portuguese army, marching into Spain. In a series of battles over the next five years, he liberated all of Spain from Napoleonic rule and, in early 1814, had crossed the French frontier and was heading north toward Paris. After Napoleon's abdication brought the war to a close, Wellington was asked to take Lord Castlereagh's place at the Congress of Vienna.

When news of Napoleon's escape from Elba reached Vienna, Wellington was recalled to the Austrian Netherlands, where he hurriedly built up an army from the surviving veterans of his campaigns in Spain. On June 18, 1815, Wellington's improvised force met and defeated Napoleon's at Waterloo. The duke supervised the occupation army that garrisoned France following the Second Treaty of Paris and later became commander in chief of the British Army. In 1828, he was made prime minister and served for two years, with a brief return in 1834. Among his political achievements was the passing of a bill granting British Catholics the right to vote. When Wellington died in 1852, he was given the almost unprecedented honor of a state funeral and was buried in a magnificent tomb in St. Paul's Cathedral, in the heart of London.

Blucher, a veteran of the 1813 war, would command the Prussian army. Arthur Wellesley, the duke of Wellington, who had defeated the French in Spain, had just arrived as Britain's representative at the Congress. He would now leave to take command of a hurriedly organized Anglo-Dutch army that was forming in the Austrian Netherlands.

The chances of the coalition's success were not considered good. Bookmakers in Vienna were offering 50-50 odds that Napoleon would beat the coalition.

"THE NEAREST RUN THING YOU EVER SAW . . ."

The delegates in Vienna were right. Napoleon had no intention of waiting for the forces of the Sixth Coalition to engulf him. When he heard the news that he had been made an international outlaw, Bonaparte immediately began building an army. By a miracle of improvisation, he was soon in command of almost 200,000 men, many of them experienced veterans of his old campaigns. True to his aggressive nature, he decided to attack the Allied forces mustering to the northeast before they could attack him. On June 15, 1815, he crossed the frontier and invaded the Austrian Netherlands.

Napoleon hoped to keep Blucher and Wellington's forces separated and attack them individually, thereby denying them the opportunity to use their greater numbers together—a tactic known as "defeat in detail." Outfoxing his opponents initially, Bonaparte pounced on the Prussian army and gave it a severe beating at the Battle of Ligny. Then he turned north and marched up the main road toward Brussels, the capital of the Austrian Netherlands. On his journey northwards, he ran straight into Wellington's army blocking his way just outside the town of Waterloo. On the morning of June 18, Napoleon launched his assault.

The battle lasted all day. Bonaparte's 250 cannons blasted the positions of the Anglo-Dutch army, which was dug in just behind a shallow ridge. His infantry and cavalry charged at

A portrait of the Duke of Wellington, the British commander who routed Napoleon's forces at the Battle of Waterloo on June 18, 1815. Wellington's victory brought Napoleon's Hundred Days to an end and exiled the former French emperor to the island of St. Helena in the middle of the South Atlantic Ocean.

Wellington's defensive line throughout the morning and afternoon. At the center of the battlefield, a furious fight took place to seize a farmhouse that was critical to Wellington's position.

BONAPARTE GOES INTO HIS FINAL EXILE

Even during his imprisonment in England before his final journey to the lonely island of St. Helena, Napoleon Bonaparte remained defiant. Large crowds came to watch him—a figure of enormous charisma and fascination—as he paced the deck of his prison ship, as this account by his Irish doctor, Barry O'Meara, indicates:

> At this period Bonaparte was represented to have been very fat. He was dressed in a plain green coat with a red collar; the coat buttoned close on the breast, cut in the usual French fashion. . . . His complexion was represented to be clear; his eyes black, rather small, fixed, steady and impressive; his chin very prominent, his hair a jet black, and his lips small, forming altogether an agreeable and pleasing countenance. He was rather bald upon the head, and had no whiskers. . . .
>
> He spent much time in walking the deck, and intentionally exposed himself every evening, to gratify the immense crowds who came to see him. "Is this he—is this the man who has made and unmade kings—who has so wasted and destroyed the human species?" was the exclamation of thousands who carne to see the great sight. "He is nothing but a man," said some; others said they discovered no marks of greatness. "How should this man have bestrode the world?" was the remark of some. . . .

At one point, the outcome of the whole battle hung in the balance when a giant French soldier wielding an ax broke through the farmhouse's main gate and almost managed to secure a

On the 6th of August [1815] Sir Henry Dunbury and Mr. Bathurst came on board to communicate to him the decision of the allied sovereigns as to his final destiny. He received the information, that he was to be transported to the Island of St. Helena, with only four of his friends and twelve of his servants, without surprise or agitation, having been previously appraised of the determination. He however protested against it with great emphasis, and urged his objections with great coolness, self-possession, energy and eloquence, in a speech of three quarters of an hour. . . .

Napoleon protested with great vehemence against the conduct of the British government in making a prisoner of a man who had voluntarily sought an asylum under their laws. . . . A British officer standing near observed, that if he had not been sent to St. Helena, he would have been delivered up to the emperor of Russia. To this Bonaparte observed, "God keep me from the Russians," shrugging up his shoulders. "At what hour tomorrow," said Sir George Cockburn, "shall I come, general, and receive you on board the Northumberland?" "At ten o'clock," said Bonaparte, manifesting some surprise at being styled merely *general*. . . .

Thus the man, who once had a Senate at his heels, and immense armies at his command; who was surrounded by all the courtiers, flatterers, office-seekers and parasites of an empire, was now reduced to the retinue of four personal friends and a dozen servants. How were the mighty fallen! What wonderful vicissitudes in the fortune of an individual.*

* Barry O'Meara, *Memoirs of the Military and Political Life of Napoleon Bonaparte* (Hartford, Conn.: Chauncey Goodrich, 1822).

bridgehead for his comrades; he was thrown back only by a heroic countercharge. By late afternoon, it was starting to look as though Wellington's army would break under the strain. Then, however, to Bonaparte's dismay, Blucher's Prussian forces, which he had thought were too badly mauled to return to the fight, appeared to the French rear. In desperation, Bonaparte launched one final assault using his bravest troops, the Imperial Guard, but the disciplined fire of the British infantry threw them back. The French Army began to disintegrate in panic and disorder. By evening it was all over.

Wellington made no secret of how close the outcome had been. "Blucher and I have lost 30,000 men," he told one of his fellow officers. It was, he said, "the nearest run thing you ever saw in your life."[3]

THE SECOND TREATY OF PARIS

Bonaparte fled the battlefield of Waterloo but was captured a few days later. Louis XVIII returned sheepishly to Paris from his hideaway in the Austrian Netherlands shortly afterward. With the collapse of the brief second Napoleonic Empire, a new peace treaty had to be drawn up in Vienna. Though Talleyrand had managed to place the blame for the Hundred Days squarely on the Corsican's shoulders, France did not get away scot-free. The terms of the Second Treaty of Paris, as it became known, were harsher than the first. France lost more border territory and had to give up some important frontier fortresses. Louis's government was obliged to pay 700 million francs in compensation to the Allies, and an army of occupation was to garrison France for the next three years to make sure that there was no further mischief from Bonaparte's generals. Also, the stolen art treasures that the Sixth Coalition had turned a blind eye to the previous year now had to be returned to their original owners.

As for Napoleon himself, this time the Allies were not at all in a generous mood. There would be no cozy exile on a pleasant Mediterranean island. Bonaparte was sentenced to permanent imprisonment on the remote South Atlantic island of St. Helena, an almost uninhabited rocky pinnacle swept by the harsh oceanic winds. He would spend the remaining six years of his life there, his mind haunted by the might-have-beens of his glorious but tragic life.

First Challenges to the Congress System

The Congress of Vienna did not only deal with territorial matters. A number of committees met during the conference to discuss other issues of importance to the European powers. There was, for instance, a committee that drew up regulations about the taxation of goods traveling down international rivers such as the Rhine. Another committee was given the task of estimating the number of people who lived in various European states; in 1815, the science of demography, or the study of population, was still in its infancy and little hard data was available.

One cause that was dear to the heart of men such as Lord Castlereagh was the abolition of the slave trade. For three hundred years, as many as 12 million men, women, and children had been transported from West Africa to the plantations of the

A portrait of Foreign Secretary Robert Stewart, Viscount Castlereagh, circa 1817. A British statesman who was central to maintaining the coalition that defeated Napoleon, he was also a strong abolitionist who sought to end the slave trade among the European powers.

Americas. This trafficking in human misery had brought great wealth to Europe in its heyday, but by the turn of the nineteenth century, it was becoming increasingly unacceptable on moral grounds. In 1807, thanks to the vigorous efforts of British MP William Wilberforce and other Christian evangelicals who were appalled by slavery, Great Britain had banned the trade. Now, it urged the other members of the Congress of Vienna to do the same. Progress was slow—some European countries still made good profits from slave trafficking and were in no hurry to abandon the practice, while others, such as Austria, had little interest in the issue. Still, Castlereagh did manage to obtain a joint statement from the Congress leaders condemning the slave trade. At the end of the conference, a committee continued to collect statistics and make reports on the problem.

These committees, which dealt only with matters of secondary importance to most of the European powers, were the only permanent institutions that were established by the Congress of Vienna. There was no settled meeting place where talks between the different states could continue, no debating chamber or parliament to which they could send representatives, no staff appointed to keep records or manage correspondence. Aside from the specific treaties dealing with France's punishment and the changes to frontiers, all that emerged from the Congress after its members departed in November 1815 was a vague understanding that the great powers should continue to meet from time to time to discuss matters of international importance.

So although there was considerable agreement in 1815 that from now on diplomacy should be handled differently, nobody had defined exactly what those differences should be. This would prove to be a major handicap for statesmen in the years to come. It soon turned out that the British, for instance, thought that the Congress System should operate in a very different way than what the Austrians and the Russians wanted.

A QUADRUPLE ALLIANCE OR A HOLY ALLIANCE?

So far as Lord Castlereagh was concerned, the heart of the Congress System lay in the Quadruple Alliance, signed on November 20, 1815. As its name suggests, this alliance consisted of four powers—Britain, Russia, Prussia, and Austria—and it was intended to be a peacetime continuation of the Sixth Coalition. Under the terms of the Quadruple Alliance, which was to last for 20 years, each of the members agreed to enforce the terms of the Second Treaty of Paris and planned to meet occasionally to debate pressing diplomatic issues.

The agreement that created the Quadruple Alliance was a practical, but limited, document. It spelled out certain duties that the signatories had to abide by, but it did not attempt to transform the nature of European politics. Castlereagh assumed that diplomacy between the different powers would go on as normal. He took it for granted that at the end of the 20 years there might be some alterations to the Quadruple Alliance and that the frontiers established at the Congress of Vienna would not necessarily go unchanged. Most important, Castlereagh did not believe that the Quadruple Alliance should become some sort of antirevolutionary police force. Like many Britons, he had some sympathies for the liberals and nationalists in continental Europe and believed it was neither moral nor realistic to suppress them forever. The internal affairs of each state were its own business, he concluded, and no one else's.

Two months before the signing of the Quadruple Alliance, however, Czar Alexander I had launched an initiative of his own. He had written to all the crowned rulers of Europe and asked them to join what he called a "Holy Alliance" of Christian monarchs. The terms of this alliance were extremely vague; Alexander asked his fellow monarchs to "remain united by the bonds of a true and indissoluble fraternity," to "lend each other aid and assistance," and to "protect religion, peace, and justice."[1] What any of this actually meant in practical terms was a mystery, but most of Europe's rulers signed so as not to offend the czar. Metternich privately thought that the Holy Alliance was nonsensical and that Alexander was a religious fanatic. He also saw, cunningly, that he

ROBERT STEWART, LORD CASTLEREAGH (1769–1822)

Lord Castlereagh is probably better known today for the gruesome circumstances of his suicide in 1822 than he is for his diplomatic achievements. For 10 years, Castlereagh effectively managed Britain's foreign interests, helping to create the Sixth Coalition that defeated Napoleon and accomplishing most of his country's goals at the Congress of Vienna. He was reviled by many during his lifetime because of his supposedly narrow-minded ideals. While Castlereagh was certainly conservative in his later years, he rejected some of the more extreme measures proposed by Metternich and his principled refusal to agree to the Troppau Protocol in 1820 led to Britain's withdrawal from the Congress System.

Castlereagh was born in Dublin, Ireland, the son of a wealthy landowner with prestigious family connections throughout the British Empire, including India. In 1794, he became a member of the House of Commons. Three years later, he was made chief secretary of Ireland. His time in office was a turbulent one; in 1798, a rebellion broke out among Irish Catholics angry at their treatment by the British government. Castlereagh helped to suppress the revolt, but he was sympathetic toward many of the rebels' complaints and lobbied to create a full political union between Britain and Ireland, which he believed would be the only way to appease the Irish. Unfortunately for Castlereagh, he promised Irish Catholic

might be able to exploit it for his own purposes. In the years to come, the clash between the principles of the Quadruple Alliance and the Holy Alliance would break apart the Congress System.

leaders that if they supported the Act of Union they would be allowed to vote in the British Parliament, something his colleagues in the government had no intention of permitting. Stung by this betrayal, Castlereagh resigned his post in protest.

A few years later, Castlereagh returned to office, serving initially as secretary of state for War and the Colonies. During this time, he became involved in a series of increasingly violent disputes with Foreign Secretary George Canning, the man who would become Castlereagh's fiercest rival. In 1809, the dispute between the two became so vicious that Castlereagh challenged Canning to a duel. Canning, who had never fired a pistol in his life, was almost killed, and the scandal of two government ministers shooting at one another in a public place was so great that both were made to resign. In 1812, however, Castlereagh was back, this time holding Canning's old job at the Foreign Office.

At the Congress of Vienna, Castlereagh persuaded the other European powers to hand over Antwerp and the other ports of the Low Countries (which were vital to British naval security) to the neutral Kingdom of Holland. The Quadruple Alliance that he helped create defended Britain from any revival of French aggression. Castlereagh, however, did not wish to see the Alliance suppressing liberal ideas across the continent. Unpopular among the British public because of his association with Metternich, Castlereagh suffered from increasingly violent mood swings. In 1821, he had a nervous breakdown; the following year, in a fit of suicidal depression, he slit his own throat with a letter opener. It was a sad end for a man who had achieved so much for his country.

THE TROPPAU PROTOCOL

This clash of principles did not become apparent until the Troppau Conference, which was held in November 1820 in what is today the town of Opava in the Czech Republic.

In the five years between the end of the Congress of Vienna and the meeting in Troppau, the system worked fairly smoothly. In 1818, the powers met for the first time at Aix-la-Chapelle (nowadays known as Aachen), on the German border with France, to review the Second Treaty of Paris. The peace settlement had gone well. Louis XVIII had paid off the 700 million francs compensation in full, and it was clear that his subjects were weary of Napoleonic adventures. As a reward, the allies decided to end their military occupation and invited France to become a member of the Quadruple Alliance (turning it into the Quintuple Alliance). This was a triumph for Talleyrand. Not only was France no longer being punished, but it had also been elevated to the status of full partner with the other victors of Vienna.

So far, so good. Then, however, in 1820, liberal revolutions broke out in Spain; Portugal; and Naples, Italy. From Austria's point of view, the last was the most dangerous, because if the liberals were successful in southern Italy then they might threaten Austria's dominance in the north. Metternich had already devoted much time to suppressing revolutionary threats. The previous year he had gotten the German Confederation to pass a series of restrictions on freedom of speech in German colleges and universities—the so-called Carlsbad Decrees—because he thought liberal and nationalist professors and students were stirring up trouble. Now he wanted to use the Holy Alliance to crush the Neapolitan revolution.

Czar Alexander, who had started out his reign as something of a liberal himself, was by this time deeply influenced by Metternich. He agreed to a resolution at the meeting at Troppau that authorized members of the Holy Alliance to intervene by force if a fellow monarch was threatened by revolution. "States which have undergone a change of government due to revolution . . . cease to be members of the European Alliance," the protocol read. "If, owing to such alterations, immediate danger threatens other states, the powers bind themselves, by peaceful means, or if need be, by arms, to bring back the guilty state into the bosom of the Great Alliance."[2]

Metternich used the power authorized by the Troppau Protocol quickly. In 1821, a large Austrian force marched into Naples and smashed the small liberal army there. The British, however, were outraged. This was not what the Congress System was supposed to be about. After Troppau, Great Britain increasingly distanced itself from the other members of the Quintuple Alliance.

REVOLUTIONS IN GREECE & LATIN AMERICA

Lord Castlereagh never recovered from the disappointment of Troppau. Regardless of his sympathies with the liberals and nationalists, the British public blamed him for Metternich's actions. Depressed, the foreign secretary committed suicide in 1822. Castlereagh was replaced by George Canning, an old rival, who was even more opposed to Metternich's policies than his predecessor had been.

Despite his victory at Troppau, Metternich would soon find out that other revolutions would not be so easily dealt with as the Neapolitan one. The first took place in Greece, a Christian country that for centuries had been governed by the Muslim Otttoman Empire. In 1821, Greek nationalists rebelled, demanding a state of their own. As civil war broke out, the Ottoman forces brutally suppressed the Greeks. Although the Ottomans were not part of the Congress System, Metternich thought that no good could come from encouraging a nationalist revolution. Alexander I, however, was much more conflicted. After all, it seemed distasteful for the Christian Holy Alliance to stand by and watch fellow Christians be massacred.

(continues on page 88)

THE MONROE DOCTRINE (1823)

On December 2, 1823, President James Monroe of the United States gave his annual State of the Union address in Washington, D.C. In it, Monroe warned the European powers that the United States would no longer tolerate foreign interference in North or South America. The speech was the first bold declaration that the United States regarded itself as the guardian of the Western Hemisphere, and that future attempts at colonization in the Americas would be met with resistance. It was, in that sense, an act of defiance toward the Congress System. Here is an excerpt from Monroe's address:

> The American continents, by the free and independent condition which they have assumed and maintain, are henceforth not to be considered as subjects for future colonization by any European powers. . . .
>
> The citizens of the United States cherish sentiments the most friendly in favor of the liberty and happiness of their fellow-men on that side of the Atlantic. In the wars of the European powers in matters relating to themselves we have never taken any part, nor does it comport with our policy to do so. It is only when our rights are invaded or seriously menaced that we resent injuries or make preparation for our defense. . . .
>
> The political system of the [Congress] powers is essentially different in this respect from that of America. This difference proceeds from that which exists in their respective Governments; and to the defense of our own, which has been achieved by the loss of so much blood and treasure, and matured by the wisdom of their most enlightened citizens, and under which we

have enjoyed unexampled felicity, this whole nation is devoted. We owe it, therefore, to candor and to the amicable relations existing between the United States and those powers to declare that we should consider any attempt on their part to extend their system to any portion of this hemisphere as dangerous to our peace and safety. . . .

It is impossible that the [Congress] powers should extend their political system to any portion of either continent without endangering our peace and happiness; nor can anyone believe that our southern brethren, if left to themselves, would adopt

James Monroe was the fifth president of the United States, serving from 1817 to 1825. He established the U.S. policy of noninterference by Europeans in the Americas that has come to be known as the Monroe Doctrine.

it of their own accord. It is equally impossible, therefore, that we should behold such interposition in any form with indifference. If we look to the comparative strength and resources of Spain and those new Governments, and their distance from each other, it must be obvious that she can never subdue them. It is still the true policy of the United States to leave the parties to themselves, in hope that other powers will pursue the same course.*

* "Monroe Doctrine," December 2, 1823, The Avalon Project, Yale Law School. http://avalon.law.yale.edu/19th_century/monroe.asp.

(continued from page 85)

Also, the Russians had a self-interested reason to intervene on the side of the Greeks: They were eager to expand their influence southward into the eastern Mediterranean region.

The other revolts that shook the Congress System took place halfway around the world, in Latin America. The Spanish and Portuguese colonies in the Americas had been inspired by the events of the French Revolution to seek their own independence. Mexico began the process by breaking free of Spanish control in 1810; then, one by one, Venezuela, Paraguay, Chile, Argentina, and other states of the old colonial empire declared their independence. In 1822, Portugal lost Brazil. Both Spain and Portugal (egged on by Metternich) wanted to reassert their control of their rebellious colonies, but since Great Britain's Royal Navy controlled the sea lanes, any attempt at quashing the revolutions would require Britain's cooperation, and this Canning refused to give. Britain and the United States were informally united on this issue. In 1823, the American president, James Monroe, announced in his now-famous Monroe Doctrine that his country would no longer tolerate foreign interference in the Americas. As a result, the conservatives in Europe had little choice but to watch the Spanish and Portuguese overseas empires crumble.

The Congress System Collapses

"Europe is involved in a crisis. . . . I foresaw the event; I have combated it consistently during a ministry of well-nigh forty years. To check the torrent is no longer within the power of man. . . . *[M]y efforts have been in vain.*"[1] Klemens Wenzel von Metternich, writing here to the Russian czar, was acknowledging the crumbling of the world he had fought so painstakingly to preserve. On March 13, 1848, a mob of angry Viennese citizens had surrounded the foreign minister's elegant townhouse and demanded his resignation. The Austrian capital was, like most of Europe's great cities, in revolutionary turmoil that spring. A liberal and nationalist wave had surged over the continent, threatening to engulf the conservative monarchs who still preserved the old order of 1815. Metternich was one of the first casualties. After almost 40 years of uninterrupted steerage of Austria's diplomacy, the aging statesman was forced to resign his office and retreat into exile in England.

Metternich had long predicted his own fall. He had become increasingly convinced that the Congress System he had tried to implement after Napoleon's abdication was doomed to failure. In some ways, Metternich was being unnecessarily pessimistic. Europe would still enjoy more than a half century of relative peace after 1848. The ideological trend, however, was unmistakable—conservatives now had to adjust to the realities of popular liberalism and nationalism, or die.

THE BEGINNING OF THE END?

In 1825, Czar Alexander I died suddenly and mysteriously. His passing was to have major repercussions for the Congress System. Alexander's successor, his brother Nicholas I, was certainly no liberal sympathizer, but neither was he inspired by the same religious mysticism as the former czar had been. His foreign policy would be based strictly on Russia's self-interest rather than the ideology of the Holy Alliance. Metternich had lost his closest ally among the crowned heads of Europe. While his older brother had procrastinated for years over the fate of the Greeks, who were still in revolt against the Ottoman Empire, Nicholas instead took bold action. Assisted by the British and French, who had been appalled by the brutal treatment of the Greek rebels, Russian forces smashed the Turkish army and forced the Ottoman emperor to sue for peace. In 1829, Greece won its independence at last.

Just a year later came the first in a series of revolutionary earthquakes that were to shake Europe for the rest of the nineteenth century. To begin with, France's last Bourbon king, Charles X, who had succeeded Louis XVIII, was overthrown, and a replacement monarch, Louis-Philippe, was put in his place. To secure his position, Louis-Philippe promised to introduce a liberal constitution to France and to govern with the consent of parliament. That same year, the citizens of the for-

An 1815 portrait of Prince Klemens Wenzel von Metternich, who was one of the key architects of the Congress System that maintained the balance of power in Europe after Napoleon's final defeat. He was widely admired for the way in which he negotiated compromises among the great powers.

mer Austrian Netherlands rose up in revolt against the king of Holland. As Catholics, they had never been particularly keen on being united with their Protestant neighbors in the north, and the Dutch government had not handled the annexation very sensitively. Because the coupling of the Austrian Netherlands to Holland had been one of Britain's major demands at the Congress of Vienna, Britons were not surprisingly alarmed to see the region in the midst of revolution. The British government, however, eventually realized that the two lands could not be peacefully reunited, and so supported the creation of the new kingdom of Belgium. This was the first, but far from the last, territorial change to the settlement of 1815.

1848: THE SPRINGTIME OF NATIONS

After 1830, Europe again entered a period of relative stability. The forces of popular liberalism and nationalism, however, were swelling despite the apparent calm. Economic crisis would be the key ingredient that would spark revolutionary fervor. In the mid-1840s, the continent was devastated by a series of famines. Millions, from Ireland to Poland, died of starvation. Too many of Europe's conservative governments were incapable of helping their hungry subjects or seemed indifferent to their plight. Resentment began to bubble to the surface.

In the spring of 1848, the economic crisis turned political. Popular revolts broke out spontaneously in almost all of Europe's capital cities. In France, Louis-Philippe, who had been a disappointment as a constitutional monarch, was unseated and a new republic was declared. In Austria, as we have seen, Metternich was deposed. The revolutionaries wanted liberal constitutions, but many of them also sought national rights as well. Italian and German radicals demanded the creation of unified states. The Hungarians, who were part of the Austrian Empire, revolted, claiming a state of their own. It was, as the phrase went, the "springtime of nations." The revolutionary mood seemed as electric as that of 1789.

In the short term, however, the liberals and nationalists were defeated. The conservative rulers, who initially were frightened by the revolt of their subjects, regained their confidence after a few months. The German and Italian nationalists were brought to heel. Nicholas I helped to suppress the Hungarians. In France, the nephew of Napoleon Bonaparte deposed the republic and declared himself emperor (but reassured his fellow monarchs that he wanted only peace). Even Metternich was able to return to Vienna, though he never regained political office and died a few years later.

So it seemed at first as though the Congress System had prevailed. In reality, however, an important and permanent change had taken place. Despite regaining control of their kingdoms, most of the European monarchs agreed to create or maintain some kind of liberal constitution. The more perceptive conservative politicians, such as Prussia's Otto von Bismarck, could see that nationalism was the future: Germany was going to be united eventually no matter what, so conservatives needed to use nationalist ideology for their own purposes rather than oppose it. The days of simply trying to suppress all radical ideology were over.

ITALIAN AND GERMAN NATIONHOOD

Neither Italy nor Germany was unified because of the efforts of nationalist radicals. They were unified because two conservative monarchs in Piedmont and Prussia decided to use the power of nationalism for their own purposes and were able to implement their will by force.

Piedmont was a medium-sized kingdom in the northwestern part of the Italian peninsula. When revolution broke out across Italy in 1848, including in the Austrian-controlled regions of Venetia and Lombardy, the king of Piedmont attempted to exploit the situation by leading a patriotic "war of liberation" against the Austrians. While this ended in battlefield disaster for the luckless Piedmontese, they learned that in any future war against Austria they would need the support of another of the great European powers. In 1859, they gained this help in the form of France. With French military assistance,

OTTO VON BISMARCK (1815–1898)

If the years between the Congress of Vienna and the 1848 revolutions were effectively the Age of Metternich, the 50 years that followed became indisputably the Age of Bismarck. Unifier of the German Empire and creator of the alliance system that would ultimately drag the great powers to war in 1914, Otto von Bismarck was the conservative genius who exploited liberal and national ideas for his own purposes, who conquered Prussia's enemies while at the same time introducing universal male suffrage and the welfare state.

Bismarck, the son of a minor Prussian nobleman, was born on his family estate west of Berlin at the same time the Congress of Vienna was sitting. After a few years as a lawyer and in military service, the young Bismarck returned home to run its estates. In 1847, he won a place in Prussia's aristocratic parliament, where he gained a reputation as a hardline conservative. When he heard that King Frederick William IV had bowed to a revolutionary mob in Berlin and had agreed to grant the Prussian people a constitution, Bismarck rushed to the capital to assist his monarch. This show of loyalty won him a place as Prussia's representative in the Diet of the German Confederation.

In 1861, Bismarck was appointed Prussian prime minister. Prussia's parliament, which had been reorganized after the 1848 revolution and was now dominated by middle-class liberals, was refusing to authorize funds for the army unless

Piedmont was able to drive the Austrians out of the whole of northern Italy. Then, to everyone's surprise, a revolutionary army led by the famous nationalist hero Giuseppe Garibaldi

further constitutional reforms were introduced. Bismarck ignored the protests and simply governed without parliamentary approval for four years. The thankful king came to rely on his prime minister completely. By this time, however, Bismarck was more than just a reactionary conservative. He cleverly saw that he could split the parliamentary liberals by appealing to their nationalist sentiments and offering them a unification of Germany—on Bismarck's own terms, of course.

To do this, however, he needed to remove the opposition of Austria. After a series of contrived diplomatic clashes, Bismarck found an excuse to declare war in 1866. The small but supremely well-trained and professional Prussian army swiftly destroyed Austria's less disciplined forces. After swallowing up most of northern Germany in the peace negotiations, Bismarck then turned his attention toward France. In 1870, he fought another short and victorious war against Emperor Napoleon III. In January 1871, flush with military success, the remaining south German states agreed to create a Prussian-dominated German Empire ruled by the king of Prussia, who was henceforth promoted to kaiser, or emperor. Bismarck became chancellor of the new German empire and governed with almost no opposition for the next 20 years.

In 1888, however, a young and brash new kaiser, William II, had risen to the throne and sought to govern by himself. After two years of conflict with the crown, Bismarck resigned from office, never to return. He spent the last years of his life in bitter exile on the family estate, prophesying—all too accurately as it turned out—that William II's desire for glory would one day lead to disaster for Germany.

A black-and-white portrait of Prince Otto von Bismarck, circa 1870. As Prussian prime minister, Bismarck helped to unify most of the German-speaking territories in Europe and established the German Empire in 1871.

landed in the south of the peninsula and defeated the Kingdom of Naples. Piedmont's army marched to meet Garibaldi's forces and the great revolutionary general handed over his liberated territory personally to King Victor Emmanuel. Somewhat to their astonishment, the Piedmontese had conquered almost all of Italy within a few months. The new Kingdom of Italy was declared on March 17, 1861.

German's unification took somewhat longer. The genius behind this project was Prime Minister Otto von Bismarck of Prussia. In a series of three wars, against Denmark, Austria, and France, between 1864 and 1870, he compelled or persuaded all of the members of the German Confederation to join in a single imperial union, with Prussia's King William I elevated to the rank of kaiser, or emperor. Bismarck was greatly aided in his plan by the fact that Prussia had become one of the great industrial powers of Europe during the mid-nineteenth century. The Rhineland, which Prussia had accepted so reluctantly in 1815 as compensation for the loss of its Polish territory, had turned out to be the greatest prize on the whole of the continent. By 1871, its coalfields and iron works had made Prussia an economic giant rivaling even Great Britain.

A EUROPE OF RIVALS AGAIN

Prussia's victory in 1871 meant a lot more than just a shift of boundaries in central Europe. It radically altered the whole equilibrium of power on the continent. In 1815, Metternich had been careful to ensure that Germany remained divided and weak. Leaving a vacuum of power at the heart of Europe meant that the western and eastern states remained in rough equilibrium with one another. Bismarck's unification of Germany, however, altered that equation completely. Now the greatest state in Europe was at its center. The other powers would inevitably react to this.

The result was the formation of two permanent rival alliances; one, known as the Triple Alliance, consisted of Germany,

Austria, and Italy, while the other, the Triple Entente, was made up of Britain, France, and Russia. It would only take a spark from an unexpected quarter to set the two sides at war with one another. Sure enough, on June 28, 1914, the heir to

THE GERMAN EMPIRE IS CREATED

On January 18, 1871, following the victorious war against France, the German states agreed to form a single united empire under the leadership of Prussia's kaiser William I. This historic moment, which would for the first time in centuries make Germany the political center of the European continent, was recorded by a patriotic German newspaper:

> In the palace of Louis XIV, in that ancient center of a hostile power which for centuries has striven to divide and humiliate Germany, the solemn proclamation of the German empire was made on January 18 [1871]. . . . Though the German people, owing to the necessities of the times, were represented at the ceremony only by the German army, the eyes of the entire nation were gratefully turned to the place where, surrounded by sovereigns, generals, and soldiers, King William announced to the world the assumption by himself and his heirs of a title for the reestablishment of which we have been yearning during the sixty long years it has been in abeyance. . . .
>
> By the self-sacrificing devotion of all classes of society, the nation has proved that it still possesses that warlike prowess which distinguished our ancestors. It has recovered its ancient position in Europe; and, neither fearing an adversary nor envying any neighbor, discreet

the Austrian throne, Franz Ferdinand, was assassinated while visiting Sarajevo, in what is now Bosnia and Herzegovina. The Austrians blamed the Kingdom of Serbia, which Russia was committed to protecting. As one power slid into war, it dragged

and temperate in its acts and aims, it accepts the destiny prophesied for it in the proclamation of its new emperor. This destiny is to add to its power not by conquest but by promoting culture, liberty, and civilization. As far as the German people are concerned, there will be no more wars in Europe after the determination of the present campaign. . . .

The crown prince, with Lieutenant-General Blumenthal, his chief of staff, and an escort of Prussians, Wurtembergers, Badeners, and Bavarians, drove to the palace to receive his royal father at the eastern portal in front of the Princes' Stairway. In the courtyard of the palace a company of the king's own troops was drawn up as a guard of honor. . . .

At a quarter past twelve his Majesty entered the hall, when a choir consisting of men of the Seventh, Forty-Seventh, and Fifty-Eighth regiments intoned the choral,

"Let all the world rejoice in the Lord. . . ."

The king then walked up to where the colors were displayed, and, standing before them, read the document proclaiming the reestablishment of the German empire. Count Bismarck having read the king's proclamation to the German nation, the grand duke of Baden stepped forth and exclaimed, "Long live his Majesty the emperor!" The cheers of the assembly were taken up by the bands playing the national anthem.*

* "The Creation of the German Empire At Versailles (1871)," Documents on European History in the Age of Revolution and Reaction. http://personal.ashland.edu/~jmoser1/german empire.htm.

all of its alliances partners in along with it. By August 4, 1914, the whole of the continent was at war in a way not seen since the days of Bonaparte. The Congress System had finally and totally collapsed. The First World War, as it became known, would continue for the next four and a half years. Approximately 10 million soldiers would die in its terrible fighting before an armistice was signed in 1918. It was the carnage of the Battle of Leipzig all over again, but this time multiplied a hundredfold.

9

A World
in Turmoil

The central gallery of the Palace of Versailles in France, known as the Hall of Mirrors, has been the location of many dramatic events in the past two centuries. In October 1789, a few months after the outbreak of the French Revolution, this magnificent arched enclosure was invaded by angry peasants who kidnapped Louis XVI and dragged him and his family 13 miles (20.9 kilometers) back to Paris. In January 1871, it was the site of the inauguration of the German Empire. In June 1919, it was chosen to be the place in which the victorious Allied powers—chiefly France, Great Britain, Italy, and the United States—would sign the peace treaty ending the great world war they had just fought against that empire.

The Treaty of Versailles, however, as it became known, was intended to be more than simply an end to the war. It was

(continues on page 104)

WOODROW WILSON
(1856–1924)

Following the armistice ending World War I, Woodrow Wilson, the twenty-eighth president of the United States, believed that future war could be avoided only by rein-stituting a system of diplomatic mediation along the lines of the Congress of Vienna. This time, however, it would be in the shape of a permanent legal body, with repre-sentatives from across the world, committed to liberal principles rather than illiberal ones. It was a bold vision, and one that tragically fell far short of expectations. "Wilsonian ideals" of international cooperation, however, would continue to excite minds throughout the twentieth century, and would eventually come to fruition in the form of the United Nations.

Wilson was born in Staunton, Virginia, the son of a Presbyterian clergyman and professor of theology. After earning a doctorate at The Johns Hopkins University in 1885, Wilson taught history and politics at several colleg-es. He rose to become president of Princeton University in 1902. In 1910, he won the governorship of New Jersey. After just two years in office, Wilson was offered the national Democratic Party's candidacy in the 1912 presi-dential election. Former president Theodore Roosevelt's decision to run on a third-party ticket that year split the Republican vote, and Wilson won handsomely.

Although he had not previously expressed any strong views about foreign policy, Wilson's time in office quickly came to be dominated by international affairs when the

First World War broke out in Europe in 1914. Although sympathetic to the cause of Britain and France, Wilson was initially determined to keep the United States out of the war and worked strenuously to negotiate peace between the two sides as a neutral honest broker. In November 1916, he won reelection to the White House using the slogan "He Kept Us Out of the War." The following spring, however, Germany began unrestricted submarine attacks against American shipping, a provocation too blatant to ignore. Wilson declared war. While mobilizing American manpower and industry, the president announced an ambitious series of postwar goals which became known as his "Fourteen Points." These included the creation of the League of Nations, a worldwide forum for peaceful diplomacy. In early 1919, following Germany's defeat, Wilson left the United States to spend six months in Europe discussing the peace treaty and the establishment of the League of Nations. In Paris, he was greeted as a hero and addressed admiring crowds of thousands.

Popularity abroad could not guarantee success at home, however. Congress rejected the peace treaty and refused to join Wilson's proposed league, fatally crippling it. Shortly after returning to the United States, Wilson suffered a debilitating stroke and spent the remaining period of his presidential term almost totally incapacitated, his wife effectively running the administration in his place. He died soon after leaving office.

In one of last addresses to the League of Nations in September 1919, Wilson had predicted that another world war would occur if the nations of the world did not cooperate to prevent it. Sadly, Wilson's prophecy came true 20 years later.

Representatives to the League of Nations are photographed during an assembly meeting in Geneva, Switzerland, in 1920. Though ultimately a failed experiment, the League had its roots in the international cooperation seen in the Congress of Vienna.

(continued from page 101)
intended to be an end to war itself. The Allied statesmen assembled there wanted nothing less than to re-create the kind of lasting peace settlement that Metternich had masterminded in 1815. The Congress System had, for all its faults, largely maintained peace in Europe for a century. The steady breakdown of that system after 1871, and the formation of two dueling alliances in place of a stable balance of power, was held respon-

sible for the terrible world war that had followed. Just as the continent's diplomats had yearned for security after the fall of Napoleon Bonaparte, their successors in 1919 sought it as well.

Unfortunately, the security institution created to preserve the peace, known as the League of Nations, did not succeed. Barely 20 years after the signing of the peace treaty in Versailles' Hall of Mirrors, Europe was again embroiled in an even more terrible world war. When World War II finally ended in 1945, it was time once more to try to create a stable international order. Hopes were placed in the United Nations, the successor to the League of Nations. In the decades since its founding in 1945, the United Nations, though far from perfect, has been more successful as a forum for the international community and an arbiter of diplomatic disputes. Many of the basic problems, however, that Metternich and the other delegates faced in Vienna at the end of the Napoleonic Wars continue today. How can stability be ensured in a world that continues to be rocked by turbulent political and ideological changes?

THE ROAD TO WORLD WAR II

The League of Nations was a bold experiment. The peacemakers at Versailles wanted to avoid some of the problems they felt had dogged the Vienna settlement in 1815, especially the lack of any permanent assembly or meeting place. The League was intended to be a sort of global debating chamber in which representatives from all the world's nations could discuss and negotiate mutual disagreements without having to resort to the kind of bloodshed that had been seen during the First World War. The emphasis would be on *open* discussions, with no voices excluded—a break from the diplomacy of the nineteenth century, in which it was argued that too many of Europe's key decisions had been made behind closed doors by the largest four or five great powers without consulting the smaller states.

One problem with the League of Nations, however, was that a number of major countries were not represented within it, either because they had been deliberately excluded or because they had chosen not to take part. Germany, for instance, was left out at first as punishment for having lost the war. The Soviet Union was not initially asked to join because the Bolshevik revolutionaries who had taken over Russia in 1917 were not considered respectable politicians. Perhaps most crucially, the United States was not a member, despite President Woodrow Wilson having inspired the idea of the League in the first place. In 1919, the U.S. Congress decisively rejected the idea of inclusion, arguing that membership would compromise America's longstanding isolationist policy. The lack of an American presence in the League of Nations was keenly felt. By the end of World War I, the United States was the richest and arguably the strongest of the world's great powers, and so its absence from the League left a vacuum at the heart of the organization.

Moreover, because any major decision regarding the League had to be ratified by all of the representatives on its 15-member ruling council, it was extremely hard to find agreement on any important issue. This became obvious in the 1930s when the fascist states, led by a revived Germany, began acting aggressively toward their neighbors. With the League's members unable to agree amongst themselves about the appropriate response to these provocations, the organization's reputation plummeted and it came to be seen as a powerless talking shop. By the time war broke out again in September 1939, the League was more or less defunct.

A NEW WORLD ORDER: THE UNITED NATIONS

The Second World War lasted six years and was even more catastrophic than the first had been. While estimates vary, at least 65 million people died in fighting across the world, many of them civilians. The war had seen not only massive suffering and destruction, but had also ended with the invention and successful use of the first atomic weapons, which destroyed the

The United Nations was founded in 1945 with the express purpose of preventing another world war. Like its predecessor, the League of Nations, this international organization has sought to facilitate international cooperation and provide a place for nations to air grievances without resorting to violence.

Japanese cities of Hiroshima and Nagasaki. Given that technology had now advanced to the stage where human beings were capable of wiping out life itself, the need for a lasting peace settlement was even greater than it had been in 1919. The result

HENRY KISSINGER

Of all the modern statesmen who have tried to derive lessons from the diplomacy of Metternich, Talleyrand, and Castlereagh, few have studied the conduct of the Congress of Vienna as carefully as Henry Kissinger. The former U.S. secretary of state and national security advisor under presidents Richard Nixon and Gerald Ford wrote his doctoral dissertation on the settlement of 1815, and Metternich's statecraft was an inspiration to Kissinger throughout his own long career in public service. In his 1995 book *Diplomacy*, Kissinger set out the challenges that modern leaders must face in trying to establish a stable international system similar to that of the Congress of Vienna:

> After the dislocations caused by the French Revolution and the Napoleonic Wars, the leaders of Europe restored the balance of power at the Congress of Vienna in 1815 and softened the brutal reliance on power by seeking to moderate international conduct through moral and legal bonds. Yet by the end of the nineteenth century, the European balance of power system returned to the principles of power politics and in a far more unforgiving environment. Facing down the adversary became the standard method of diplomacy, leading to one test of strength after another. Finally, in 1914, a crisis arose from which no-one shrank. Europe never fully recovered world leadership after the catastrophe of the First World War. The United

was the United Nations Organization, founded on October 24, 1945, shortly after the war's end.

The UN constitution was designed to continue some of the better characteristics of the League of Nations, while avoiding

States emerged as the dominant player but Woodrow Wilson soon made it clear that his country refused to play by European rules. . . .

The international system of the twenty-first century will be marked by a seeming contradiction: on the one hand, fragmentation; on the other, growing globalization. On the level of the relations among states, the new order will be more like the European state system of the eighteenth and nineteenth centuries than the rigid patterns of the Cold War. It will contain at least six major powers—the United States, Europe, China, Japan, Russia, and probably India—as well as a multiplicity of medium-sized and smaller countries. At the same time, international relations have become truly global for the first time. Communications are instantaneous; the world economy operates on all continents simultaneously. A whole set of issues has surfaced that can only be dealt with on a worldwide basis, such as nuclear proliferation, the environment, the population explosion, and economic interdependence. . . .

None of the most important countries which must build a new world order have had any experience with the multistate system that is emerging. Never before has a new world order had to be assembled from so many different perceptions, or on so global a scale. Nor has any previous order had to combine the attributes of the historic balance-of-power systems with global democratic opinion and the exploding technology of the contemporary period.*

---

* Henry Kissinger, *Diplomacy* (New York: Simon and Schuster, 1995).

its weaknesses. As with the League, representation was offered to all states and open discussion of global problems through a parliamentary-style body was encouraged. The main decisions of the organization, however, would be made by the UN Security Council, the most important members of which were the five so-called "permanent" members: the United States, Great Britain, France, the Soviet Union, and China. These permanent members possessed veto rights over all resolutions. Given that these states were the principal members of the alliance that had defeated Germany and Japan in World War II, the idea was that they ought to have a disproportionately large influence over UN actions. This would avoid (it was hoped) the hesitancy and inability to come to a decision that had so often characterized the League of Nations.

In the six decades since the formation of the UN, the organization has had mixed success. Most important, the world has been spared an apocalyptic third world war, though whether that is the result of the UN per se or because none of the nuclear-armed great powers have dared to directly challenge one another is an open debate. The UN has sent numerous peacekeeping missions to the world's trouble spots and has authorized military action against nations that have acted aggressively, such as North Korea in 1950, and Saddam Hussein's Iraq in 1990. On the other hand, the organization has been accused of being a puppet manipulated in the exclusive interests of the permanent members of the Security Council. Its failure to act in times of international human rights crises, such as in Rwanda in 1994 and in Sudan a decade later, have damaged its prestige. Certainly, when one looks today at war-torn places such as Somalia and Afghanistan, its success at ensuring world peace can only be regarded as a partial one.

THE CONGRESS, TWO CENTURIES ON

What then can we say about the Congress of Vienna almost two centuries later? Given the overwhelming triumph of the liberal and nationalist ideologies in the 200 years since the French Revolution, it is tempting to look back on the staunch reactionary conservatism of men such as Metternich and draw the conclusion that the Congress System was conceived in either foolishness or wickedness. Surely, we might think, the statesmen in Vienna could not have seriously believed that they could suppress the popular desire for democracy, the rule of law, and national self-determination. The complete failure of their attempt to suppress these ideologies does not suggest that they had much of a sense of the world's future direction.

There is some truth to this; even Metternich, after all, eventually came to believe that his efforts had all been in vain, that liberal and nationalist change was inevitable. Perhaps, however, we should not judge the Congress statesmen too harshly. They had just lived through a generation of war, revolution, turmoil, and suffering. They looked on the events of the preceding 24 years with genuine shock and horror. Their desire for peace was sincere. They sought to prevent an international system without order, in which one state preyed upon another at will and in which power was the only determinant that mattered. Their efforts to create an community of cooperative states may not have been successful in the long run; certainly, the assumption held by some of them that national borders could and should be frozen for all time was unrealistic. They did believe, however, as Winston Churchill was later to put it, that "jaw-jaw was better than war-war," and the precedent they set established a template for other international security organizations in our own time. Moreover, the Congress of Vienna was followed by more than a century of relative peace and prosperity in Europe. Given that in the years since 1914 more than 100 million men, women, and children have died through conflict and genocide on that unhappy continent, that is not an achievement to treat lightly.

CHRONOLOGY

1789   Outbreak of the French Revolution. Publication of the Declaration of the Rights of Man and of the Citizen.

1793   French King Louis XVI is executed by his own subjects. Outbreak of the revolutionary wars and the Reign of Terror in France.

1795   Napoleon Bonaparte is given command of France's Army of Italy. In a series of dazzling campaigns, he defeats France's main continental enemy, Austria.

1799   Bonaparte takes part in a coup d'état and becomes first consul of France in a three-man government.

TIMELINE

1789
Outbreak of the French Revolution. Publication of the Declaration of the Rights of Man and of the Citizen.

1804
Napoleon proclaims himself emperor of France.

1818
Congress of Aix-la-Chapelle, at which France becomes a member of the Quadruple Alliance (now renamed the Quintuple Alliance).

1789

1818

1795
Napoleon Bonaparte is given command of France's Army of Italy and defeats France's main continental enemy, Austria.

1814
Napoleon abdicates; King Louis XVIII assumes the French throne. Signing of the First Treaty of Paris. The victorious Allies convene the peace Congress in Vienna.

1815
Bonaparte returns from exile, but is defeated at the Battle of Waterloo. The Congress revises the Treaty of Paris. Creation of the Quadruple Alliance and the Holy Alliance.

1804   Napoleon proclaims himself emperor of France.

1805   At the Battle of Trafalgar, the British Royal Navy destroys any hope of France invading England. Shortly afterward, at the Battle of Austerlitz, Napoleon smashes the combined armies of Austria and Russia.

1809   Prince von Metternich becomes Austrian foreign minister.

1812   Napoleon's invasion of Russia fails disastrously.

1813   Napoleon's forces are decisively defeated by the Allied coalition at the Battle of Leipzig.

1814   Napoleon abdicates; King Louis XVIII assumes the French throne. Signing of the First Treaty of Paris. The victorious Allies convene the peace Congress in Vienna.

1820
Liberal revolutions break out in Spain, Portugal, and Italy. Congress of Troppau leads to the antirevolutionary Troppau Protocol.

1914
Outbreak of the First World War, ending the century of relative peace in Europe created by the Congress of Vienna.

1945
The United Nations is formed at the end of the Second World War.

1820

1945

1821
Greece declares independence from Ottoman Turkey. (The war ends successfully for the Greeks in 1829.) Austria intervenes to crush revolutionary activity in Italy.

1919
Treaty of Versailles ends the First World War. Creation of the League of Nations, which lasts until the outbreak of the Second World War in 1939.

1848
Revolutions break out across Europe. Metternich is deposed as Austrian foreign minister.

1815   Bonaparte returns from exile, but after a 100-day reign, he is defeated at the Battle of Waterloo. The Congress continues its business and revises the Treaty of Paris. Creation of the Quadruple Alliance and the Holy Alliance.

1818   Congress of Aix-la-Chapelle, at which France becomes a member of the Quadruple Alliance (now renamed the Quintuple Alliance).

1819   Publication of the Carlsbad Decrees, which restrict freedom of speech in German universities.

1820   Liberal revolutions break out in Spain, Portugal, and Italy. Congress of Troppau leads to the publication of the antirevolutionary Troppau Protocol.

1821   Greece declares independence from Ottoman Turkey. (The war ends successfully for the Greeks in 1829.) Austria intervenes to crush revolutionary activity in Italy.

1822   Brazil declares independence from Portugal. Lord Castlereagh commits suicide and is replaced by George Canning.

1823   Monroe Doctrine proclaimed.

1825   Death of Czar Alexander I effectively brings an end to the Quintuple Alliance and the Holy Alliance.

1830   In the "July Revolution" in France, King Charles X is overthrown and the liberal monarch Louis-Philippe is installed in his place. Belgium declares independence from the Netherlands (recognized in 1839).

1848   Revolutions break out across Europe. Metternich is deposed as Austrian foreign minister.

1849   All the previous years' liberal and national revolutions are suppressed.

1852   Napoleon III, Bonaparte's nephew, becomes emperor of France.

1861   The Kingdom of Italy is created.

1870   Following military victory against France, the German states agree to unify under Prussian leadership.

1914   Outbreak of the First World War, ending the century of relative peace in Europe created by the Congress of Vienna.

1919   Treaty of Versailles ends the First World War. Creation of the League of Nations, which lasts until the outbreak of the Second World War in 1939.

1945   The United Nations is formed at the end of the Second World War.

NOTES

CHAPTER 2

1. E.L. Higgins, ed., *The French Revolution as Told by Contemporaries* (Boston: Houghton Mifflin, 1966), pp. 272–273.
2. Richard Cobb and Colin Jones, eds., *The French Revolution: Voices from a Momentous Epoch 1789–1795* (London: Simon & Schuster, 1988), p. 95.

CHAPTER 3

1. Translated lyrics to "La Marseillaise." http://www.marseillaise.org/english/english.html.
2. Richard Cobb and Colin Jones, eds., *The French Revolution: Voices from a Momentous Epoch 1789–1795* (London: Simon & Schuster, 1988), p. 148.
3. Jean-Jacques Rousseau, *The Social Contract* (London: J.M. Dent & Sons, 1920), p. 5.
4. Stuart Joseph Woolf, *A History of Italy 1700–1860* (London: Taylor & Francis, 1979), p. 227.

CHAPTER 5

1. Tim Chapman, *The Congress of Vienna: Origins, Processes and Results* (London: Routledge, 1998), p. 38.

2. Gregor Dallas, *The Final Act: The Roads to Waterloo* (New York: Henry Holt, 1997), p. 297.

CHAPTER 6

1. Gregor Dallas, *The Final Act: The Roads to Waterloo* (New York: Henry Holt, 1997), p. 289.
2. David King, *Vienna, 1814* (New York: Harmony Books, 2008), p. 241.
3. Christopher Hibbert, *Wellington* (New York: Da Capo Press, 1999), p. 185.

CHAPTER 7

1. J.R. Robinson and Charles Beard, eds., *Readings in Modern European History*, Vol. II (Boston: Ginn, 1908), pp. 354–355.
2. Eric Wilmot, *The Great Powers, 1814–1914* (London: Taylor & Francis, 1992), p. 29.

CHAPTER 8

1. J.R. Robinson and Charles Beard, eds., *Readings in Modern European History*, Vol. II (Boston: Ginn, 1908), pp. 564–566.

BIBLIOGRAPHY

Chapman, Tim. *The Congress of Vienna: Origins, Processes and Results* (London: Routledge, 1998).

Cobb, Richard, and Colin Jones, eds. *The French Revolution: Voices from a Momentous Epoch 1789–1795* (London: Simon & Schuster, 1988).

Dallas, Gregor. *The Final Act: The Roads to Waterloo* (New York: Henry Holt, 1997).

Hibbert, Christopher. *Wellington* (New York: Da Capo Press, 1999).

Higgins, E.L., ed., *The French Revolution as Told by Contemporaries* (Boston: Houghton Mifflin, 1966).

King, David. *Vienna, 1814* (New York: Harmony Books, 2008).

Kissinger, Henry. *Diplomacy* (New York: Simon and Schuster, 1995).

Memoirs of the Military and Political Life of Napoleon Bonaparte (Hartford, Conn.: Chauncey Goodrich, 1822).

Monroe, James. "Message of President James Monroe at the commencement of the first session of the 18th Congress (The Monroe Doctrine)," December 2, 1823; Presidential Messages of the 18th Congress, ca. 12/02/1823–ca. 03/03/1825; Record Group 46; Records of the United States Senate, 1789–1990; National Archives. Available online. URL: http://avalon.law.yale.edu/19th_century/monroe.asp.

National Assembly of France. "Declaration of the Rights of Man and of the Citizen," August 26, 1789. Available online. URL: http://avalon.law.yale.edu/18th_century/rightsof.asp.

Prince von Metternich, Klemens Wenzel. *Memoirs of Prince Metternich* (New York: H. Fertig, 1970).

Robinson, J.R., and Charles Beard, eds. *Readings in Modern European History*, Vol. II (Boston: Ginn, 1908).

Rousseau, Jean-Jacques. *The Social Contract* (London: J.M. Dent & Sons, 1920).

Shoberl, Frederic. *Narrative of the Most Remarkable Events which Occurred in and Near Leipzig, Immediately Before, During, and Subsequent To, the Sanguinary Series of Engagements Between the Allied Armies and the French, from the 14th to the 19th October, 1813* (London: R. Ackermann, 1814).

Wilmot, Eric. *The Great Powers, 1814–1914* (London: Taylor & Francis, 1992).

Woolf, Stuart Joseph. *A History of Italy 1700–1860* (London: Taylor & Francis, 1979).

FURTHER RESOURCES

Arnold, James R. *The Aftermath of the French Revolution* (Breckenridge, Colo.: Twenty-First Century Books, 2008).

Chapman, Victoria L., and David Lindroth. *The Age of Revolution, 1750 to 1914* (New York: Facts On File, 2006).

Crompton, Samuel. *Waterloo* (Philadelphia: Chelsea House Publishers, 2002).

Dangerfield, George. *Defiance to the Old World: The Story Behind the Monroe Doctrine* (New York: Putnam, 1970).

Docalavich, Heather. *The History and Structure of the United Nations: Development and Function* (Philadelphia: Mason Crest Publishers, 2007).

Dunn, John M. *The Enlightenment* (San Diego: Lucent Books, 1999).

Gibbons, S.R. *International Cooperation: The League of Nations and UNO* (New York: Longman, 1992).

Greenblatt, Miriam. *Napoleon Bonaparte and Imperial France* (New York: Marshall Cavendish Benchmark, 2006).

Nardo, Don. *The French Revolution* (Detroit, Mich.: Lucent Books, 2008).

Von der Heide, John. *Klemens von Metternich* (Philadelphia: Chelsea House Publishers, 1988).

PICTURE CREDITS

INDEX

ABOUT THE AUTHOR

ALAN ALLPORT grew up in Whiston, England, and moved to the United States when he was 24. He received a doctorate in history from the University of Pennsylvania in 2007. He currently teaches at Syracuse University. In addition to writing several books for Chelsea House, he is the author of *Demobbed: Coming Home After the Second World War*, published by Yale University Press. He lives in Syracuse with his wife and their two children, Thomas and Katharine.